MW00889624

KALORIC MAXX AIR FRYER OVEN COOKBOOK 2024

2000 Days Healthy and Quick Recipes to Help You Air Fry, Roast, Dehydrate, and Rotisserie with Confidence and Ease

TINA C. SIMS

Copyright © 2024 By **TINA C. SIMS**. All rights reserved worldwide.

No part of this book may be reproduced or transmitted in any form or by any means, electronic or mechanical, including photocopying, recording, or by any information storage and retrieval system, without written permission from the publisher, except for the inclusion of brief quotations in a review.

Warning-Disclaimer:

The purpose of this book is to educate and entertain. The author or publisher does not guarantee that anyone following the techniques, suggestions, tips, ideas, or strategies will become successful. The author and publisher shall have neither liability nor responsibility to anyone with respect to any loss or damage caused, or alleged to be caused, directly or indirectly, by the information contained in this book.

This copyright notice and disclaimer apply to the entirety of the book and its contents, whether in print or electronic form, and extend to all future editions or revisions of the book. Unauthorized use or reproduction of this book or its contents is strictly prohibited and may result in legal action.

TABLE OF CONTENTS

INTRODUCTION TO THE KALORIK MAXX AIR FRYER OVEN

Welcome to the world of the Kalorik Maxx Air Fryer Oven! This innovative appliance is a game-changer in the kitchen, combining the functionality of multiple appliances into one powerful unit. With the Kalorik Maxx Air Fryer Oven, you can air fry, roast, broil, rotisserie, dehydrate, bake, toast, and even cook pizza - all in one sleek and modern appliance.

One of the standout features of the Kalorik Maxx Air Fryer Oven is its ability to deliver crispy, delicious results with little to no oil. The air frying technology uses rapid air circulation to cook your food evenly and create a crispy exterior, reminiscent of deep-frying but without the excess fat and calories. Say goodbye to greasy meals and hello to healthier alternatives that don't compromise on flavor.

But that's not all - the Kalorik Maxx Air Fryer Oven also shines as a versatile oven. With customized upper and lower heating elements, you can achieve even heat distribution for perfectly cooked results, whether you're baking a cake, roasting a chicken, or broiling a juicy steak. The large oven capacity allows you to cook meals for the whole family or accommodate larger dishes with ease.

One of my favorite features is the rotisserie setting, which rotates the included spit accessory during cooking. This not only ensures even cooking but also allows meats to roast in their own juices, developing maximum flavor and creating a mouth-watering, juicy result. Whether you're craving a perfectly roasted chicken or a succulent pork loin, the rotisserie function will become your new best friend.

The Kalorik Maxx Air Fryer Oven is also incredibly user-friendly. With its easy-to-use digital LED display and 21 presets, you can achieve foolproof cooking without guesswork. The glass French doors feature a single-hand automatic opening, preventing dripping or scalding, and a built-in auto-shutoff safety feature adds an extra layer of peace of mind.

But what really sets this appliance apart is its ability to deliver restaurant-quality results at home. From crispy chicken wings to perfectly seared steaks, the Kalorik Maxx Air Fryer Oven allows you to indulge in your favorite treats without compromising on taste or health.

In the chapters ahead, you'll discover a wide range of delicious recipes specifically crafted for the Kalorik Maxx Air Fryer Oven. From appetizers and snacks to main courses and desserts, this cookbook will guide you through the endless possibilities of this versatile appliance. Get ready to explore new flavors, experiment with techniques, and elevate your home cooking to new heights.

Whether you're a seasoned home chef or a beginner in the kitchen, the Kalorik Maxx Air Fryer Oven is about to become your new favorite cooking companion. So, let's dive in and discover the countless ways this innovative appliance can transform your culinary adventures!

OVERVIEW OF THE KALORIC MAXX AIR FRYER OVEN FEATURES

The Kaloric Maxx Air Fryer Oven is engineered to be the ultimate kitchen companion, combining cutting-edge technology with versatile functionality. This multitasking marvel is packed with features that will elevate your culinary game and simplify your cooking experience. Let's dive into the standout features that make this appliance a true game-changer.

Multi-Functionality Redefined

One of the most remarkable aspects of the Kaloric Maxx Air Fryer Oven is its ability to seamlessly transition between multiple cooking modes. It's not just an air fryer; it's a comprehensive cooking solution that can air fry, roast, bake, broil, toast, dehydrate, and even rotisserie with ease. This versatility means you can prepare a wide range of dishes, from crispy fried favorites to succulent roasts and delectable baked goods, all in one appliance.

Turbo Maxx Technology for Superior Results

At the heart of the Kaloric Maxx Air Fryer Oven lies the innovative Turbo Maxx technology. This advanced system combines customized upper and lower heating elements with an optimized airflow system and a high-performance turbo fan. The result? Evenly distributed heat and rapid air circulation, ensuring perfectly cooked results every time. Whether you're air frying, roasting, or baking, your dishes will boast a crispy exterior and a tender, juicy interior.

Spacious Interior for Family-Sized Meals

With a generous 26-quart interior capacity, the Kaloric Maxx Air Fryer Oven can accommodate larger meals with ease. Whether you're cooking a whole chicken, a 12-inch pizza, or up to 9 slices of toast, this oven has got you covered. No more cramming or overcrowding - just spacious cooking freedom for your favorite recipes.

User-Friendly Digital LED Display

Simplicity meets sophistication with the oven's digital LED display. Featuring 21 presets, you can effortlessly select your desired cooking mode with just a touch of a button. From air frying to rotisserie, the presets take the guesswork out of cooking, ensuring consistent and delicious results every time.

Elegant Design with Safety in Mind

The Kaloric Maxx Air Fryer Oven is not only a functional powerhouse but also a sleek and stylish addition to any kitchen. Its modern design, complete with glass French doors and a single-hand automatic opening mechanism, adds a touch of elegance while prioritizing safety. The auto-shutoff feature further enhances peace of mind by automatically stopping operation when the doors are open.

Versatile Accessories for Endless Possibilities

To complement its multifunctional capabilities, the Kaloric Maxx Air Fryer Oven comes equipped with a range of versatile accessories. From an air frying basket and baking tray to a rotisserie spit and rack handles, you'll have the right tools at your disposal for every culinary adventure. Additionally, specialized accessories like the bacon tray and 2-in-1 steak and dehydration tray open up new avenues for creative cooking.

With its advanced features, user-friendly design, and versatile functionality, the Kaloric

Maxx Air Fryer Oven is poised to revolutionize your kitchen. Whether you're a seasoned home chef or a busy family seeking convenient and healthy meal options, this appliance promises to deliver exceptional results time and time again.

BENEFITS OF AIR FRYING

Air frying has quickly become a culinary phenomenon, and for good reason. This innovative cooking method offers a myriad of benefits that make it a game-changer in the world of healthy and convenient meal preparation. Whether you're looking to indulge in your favorite fried treats without the guilt or simply seeking a more efficient way to cook, air frying delivers on all fronts. Let's explore the compelling advantages that have made air frying a household staple.

Drastically Reduced Fat and Calories

One of the most significant benefits of air frying is its ability to drastically reduce the amount of fat and calories in your meals. Traditional deep-frying methods rely on submerging foods in vats of hot oil, resulting in a significant intake of unhealthy fats and excess calories. Air frying, on the other hand, requires little to no oil, making it an excellent choice for those looking to maintain a balanced diet or manage their weight. By simply using a light coating or spray of oil, you can enjoy all the flavors and textures of your favorite fried foods without the guilt.

Crispy, Delicious Results

Despite the minimal use of oil, air frying delivers incredibly crispy and delicious results that rival, or even surpass, traditional frying methods. The secret lies in the rapid circulation of hot air around the food, which creates a perfectly crispy exterior while keeping the interior tender and juicy. Say goodbye to soggy, greasy textures and hello to perfectly cooked, crunchy delights that will satisfy your cravings without the heaviness.

Unmatched Versatility

Air frying is not limited to traditional fried foods like French fries and chicken wings. With the Kaloric Maxx Air Fryer Oven, you can air fry a wide variety of foods, from vegetables and meats to seafood and even baked goods. This versatility opens up a world of culinary possibilities, allowing you to experiment with new recipes and flavors while keeping your meals healthy and delicious.

Faster Cooking Times

Efficiency is another significant advantage of air frying. The combination of high-speed air circulation and precise temperature control in the Kaloric Maxx Air Fryer Oven results in faster cooking times compared to traditional ovens or frying methods. This not only saves you valuable time in the kitchen but also helps retain the natural flavors and nutrients of your ingredients by minimizing overcooking.

Easy Cleanup

Air frying eliminates the need for large amounts of oil, resulting in a cleaner cooking environment and easier cleanup. Say goodbye to the messy and potentially hazardous task of disposing of used oil. Instead, simply wipe down the non-stick surfaces of the air fryer

oven and its accessories, and you're ready for your next culinary adventure.

With its ability to create delicious, crispy meals with minimal fat and oil, unmatched versatility, faster cooking times, and easy cleanup, it's no wonder that air frying has taken the culinary world by storm. By incorporating the Kaloric Maxx Air Fryer Oven into your kitchen routine, you'll not only enjoy the benefits of air frying but also unlock a world of culinary possibilities that cater to your health-conscious lifestyle without compromising on flavor or satisfaction.

HELPFUL DO'S 'N' DON'T USING THE AIR FRYER OVEN

While the Kaloric Maxx Air Fryer Oven is designed to simplify your cooking experience, mastering a few tips and tricks can take your culinary creations to new heights. From achieving perfectly crispy textures to ensuring even cooking, these handy pointers will help you get the most out of your air fryer oven. Let's dive into the essential tips and tricks that will transform you into an air frying pro!

Preheating is Key

Just like a traditional oven, preheating your air fryer oven is crucial for achieving optimal results. Taking the time to preheat ensures that the internal temperature is evenly distributed, allowing your food to cook consistently from the moment it's placed inside. Skipping this step can lead to uneven cooking and a lack of crispiness. For best results, always preheat your air fryer oven as directed in the recipe or preset instructions.

A Little Oil Goes a Long Way

One of the beauty of air frying is that it requires little to no oil, making it a healthier alternative to traditional frying methods. However, a light coating of oil or cooking spray can enhance the crispiness and flavor of your dishes. A simple spray or brushing of oil on your ingredients before air frying can make a world of difference in achieving that perfectly crispy texture. Just be mindful of the amount you use to keep your meals on the healthier side.

Don't Overcrowd the Basket or Racks

Proper air circulation is essential for even cooking and crispy results. To ensure that hot air can flow freely around your food, avoid overcrowding the air frying basket or racks. Leave some space between each item, and if necessary, cook your food in smaller batches. Overcrowding can lead to uneven cooking, soggy spots, and a longer cooking time.

Shake, Flip, and Rotate

Like a conventional oven, air frying can sometimes result in uneven cooking if your food remains stationary. To combat this, make it a habit to shake or flip your food halfway through the cooking process. This simple step ensures that every piece is exposed to the hot air, resulting in evenly cooked and crispy goodness. For larger items like roasts or whole chickens, use the rotisserie function to achieve a perfectly cooked and evenly browned exterior.

Master the Cooking Times and Temperatures

While the presets on the Kaloric Maxx Air Fryer Oven provide a great starting point, cooking times and temperatures may vary depending on the type and quantity of food you're preparing. Don't be afraid to experiment and adjust as needed. Keep a close eye on your food during the initial cooking process, and make notes on any necessary adjustments for future reference. With a little practice, you'll soon become an expert in achieving the perfect doneness for your favorite dishes.

Keep It Clean

Regular cleaning and maintenance are essential for ensuring the longevity and efficiency of your air fryer oven. After each use, be sure to wipe down the interior and exterior surfaces, and remove any accumulated crumbs or grease from the basket and accessories. Refer to the user manual for specific cleaning instructions, as some components may be dishwasher-safe for added convenience.

By incorporating these tips and tricks into your air frying routine, you'll unlock the full potential of the Kaloric Maxx Air Fryer Oven. From achieving crispy perfection to ensuring even cooking and easy cleanup, these handy pointers will elevate your culinary skills and make air frying a seamless and enjoyable experience every time.

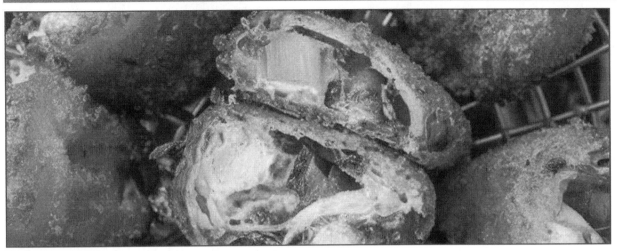

CRISPY AIR FRYER MOZZARELLA STICKS

Prep: 15 mins | Cook: 8 mins | Serves: 4

INGREDIENTS:

- 12 mozzarella string cheese sticks
- 1 cup (120g) all-purpose flour (plain flour)
- 2 large eggs, beaten
- 1 cup (100g) breadcrumbs
- 1 teaspoon Italian seasoning
- 1/2 teaspoon garlic powder
- Marinara sauce, for dipping

INSTRUCTIONS:

1. Preheat your Kaloric Maxx Air Fryer Oven to 400°F (200°C) for 3 minutes.
2. Cut the mozzarella sticks in half.
3. Dredge each mozzarella stick half in flour, then dip in beaten eggs, and finally coat with breadcrumbs mixed with Italian seasoning and garlic powder.
4. Place the coated mozzarella sticks in a single layer in the air fryer basket.
5. Air fry at 400°F (200°C) for 8 minutes, or until golden and crispy, flipping halfway through.
6. Serve hot with marinara sauce for dipping.

NUTRITIONAL INFO (PER SERVING): Calories: 320 | Fat: 15g | Carbs: 28g | Protein: 18g

Tip: Be sure not to overcrowd the air fryer basket to ensure even cooking and crispiness.

AIR FRYER BUFFALO CAULIFLOWER BITES

Prep: 10 mins | Cook: 20 mins | Serves: 4

INGREDIENTS:

- 1 head cauliflower, cut into florets
- 1/2 cup (60g) all-purpose flour (plain flour)
- 1/2 cup (120ml) milk
- 1 cup (100g) breadcrumbs
- 1 teaspoon garlic powder
- 1/2 cup (120ml) buffalo sauce
- Ranch or blue cheese dressing, for dipping

INSTRUCTIONS:

1. Preheat your Kaloric Maxx Air Fryer Oven to 375°F (190°C) for 3 minutes.
2. In a bowl, mix flour and milk to create a batter.
3. Dip each cauliflower floret into the batter, then coat with breadcrumbs mixed with garlic powder.
4. Place the coated cauliflower florets in a single layer in the air fryer basket.
5. Air fry at 375°F (190°C) for 20 minutes, shaking halfway through.
6. Toss the cooked cauliflower in buffalo sauce until well coated.
7. Serve hot with ranch or blue cheese dressing for dipping.

NUTRITIONAL INFO (PER SERVING): Calories: 180 | Fat: 5g | Carbs: 30g | Protein: 8g

Kaloric Maxx Air Fryer Oven Functions Used: Air Fry

Tip: Adjust the amount of buffalo sauce according to your desired level of spiciness.

AIR FRYER ZUCCHINI FRIES

Prep: 15 mins | Cook: 10 mins | Serves: 4

INGREDIENTS:

- 2 large zucchinis
- 1 cup (120g) all-purpose flour (plain flour)
- 2 large eggs, beaten
- 1 cup (100g) breadcrumbs
- 1/2 cup (50g) grated Parmesan cheese
- 1 teaspoon garlic powder
- Salt and pepper, to taste

INSTRUCTIONS:

1. Preheat your Kaloric Maxx Air Fryer Oven to 400°F (200°C) for 3 minutes.
2. Cut the zucchinis into fry-shaped sticks.
3. Dredge each zucchini stick in flour, then dip in beaten eggs, and finally coat with breadcrumbs mixed with Parmesan cheese, garlic powder, salt, and pepper.
4. Place the coated zucchini sticks in a single layer in the air fryer basket.
5. Air fry at 400°F (200°C) for 10 minutes, or until golden and crispy, shaking halfway through.
6. Serve hot with your favorite dipping sauce.

NUTRITIONAL INFO (PER SERVING): Calories: 220 | Fat: 8g | Carbs: 30g | Protein: 9g

Kaloric Maxx Air Fryer Oven Functions Used: Air Fry

Tip: For extra crispiness, spray a light coat of cooking oil over the zucchini fries before air frying.

AIR FRYER JALAPEÑO POPPERS

Prep: 15 mins | Cook: 8 mins | Serves: 4

INGREDIENTS:

- 8 jalapeños, halved and seeded
- 4 oz (115g) cream cheese, softened
- 1/2 cup (50g) shredded cheddar cheese
- 1/4 cup (25g) breadcrumbs
- 4 slices bacon, cooked and crumbled

INSTRUCTIONS:

1. Preheat your Kaloric Maxx Air Fryer Oven to 375°F (190°C) for 3 minutes.
2. Mix cream cheese, cheddar cheese, and bacon together in a bowl.
3. Stuff each jalapeño half with the cheese mixture.
4. Sprinkle breadcrumbs over the stuffed jalapeños.
5. Place the stuffed jalapeños in a single layer in the air fryer basket.
6. Air fry at 375°F (190°C) for 8 minutes, or until the tops are golden and the cheese is bubbly.
7. Serve hot.

NUTRITIONAL INFO (PER SERVING): Calories: 180 | Fat: 14g | Carbs: 6g | Protein: 7g

Kaloric Maxx Air Fryer Oven Functions Used: Air Fry

Tip: Adjust the amount of jalapeños based on your spice tolerance.

AIR FRYER CHICKEN NUGGETS

Prep: 15 mins | Cook: 10 mins | Serves: 4

INGREDIENTS:

- 1 lb (450g) chicken breast, cut into nugget-sized pieces
- 1 cup (120g) all-purpose flour (plain flour)
- 2 large eggs, beaten
- 1 cup (100g) breadcrumbs
- 1 teaspoon paprika
- 1/2 teaspoon garlic powder
- Salt and pepper, to taste

INSTRUCTIONS:

1. Preheat your Kaloric Maxx Air Fryer Oven to 400°F (200°C) for 3 minutes.
2. Dredge each chicken piece in flour, then dip in beaten eggs, and finally coat with breadcrumbs mixed with paprika, garlic powder, salt, and pepper.
3. Place the coated chicken pieces in a single layer in the air fryer basket.
4. Air fry at 400°F (200°C) for 10 minutes, or until golden and cooked through, shaking halfway through.
5. Serve hot with your favorite dipping sauce.

NUTRITIONAL INFO (PER SERVING): Calories: 300 | Fat: 8g | Carbs: 30g | Protein: 25g

Kaloric Maxx Air Fryer Oven Functions Used: Air Fry

Tip: Marinate the chicken pieces in buttermilk for a few hours before cooking for extra tenderness.

AIR FRYER POTATO WEDGES

Prep: 10 mins | Cook: 20 mins | Serves: 4

INGREDIENTS:

- 4 large russet potatoes
- 2 tablespoons olive oil
- 1 teaspoon garlic powder
- 1 teaspoon paprika
- Salt and pepper, to taste

INSTRUCTIONS:

1. Preheat your Kaloric Maxx Air Fryer Oven to 400°F (200°C) for 3 minutes.
2. Cut the potatoes into wedges.
3. Toss the potato wedges with olive oil, garlic powder, paprika, salt, and pepper.
4. Place the seasoned potato wedges in a single layer in the air fryer basket.
5. Air fry at 400°F (200°C) for 20 minutes, or until golden and crispy, shaking halfway through.
6. Serve hot.

NUTRITIONAL INFO (PER SERVING): Calories: 220 | Fat: 7g | Carbs: 36g | Protein: 4g

Kaloric Maxx Air Fryer Oven Functions Used: Air Fry

Tip: For extra crispiness, soak the potato wedges in water for 30 minutes before seasoning and air frying.

AIR FRYER AVOCADO FRIES

Prep: 10 mins | Cook: 8 mins | Serves: 4

INGREDIENTS:

- 2 large avocados
- 1/2 cup (60g) all-purpose flour (plain flour)
- 2 large eggs, beaten
- 1 cup (100g) breadcrumbs
- 1/4 cup (25g) grated Parmesan cheese
- 1/2 teaspoon garlic powder
- Salt and pepper, to taste

INSTRUCTIONS:

1. Preheat your Kaloric Maxx Air Fryer Oven to 375°F (190°C) for 3 minutes.
2. Cut the avocados into fry-shaped slices.
3. Dredge each avocado slice in flour, then dip in beaten eggs, and finally coat with breadcrumbs mixed with Parmesan cheese, garlic powder, salt, and pepper.
4. Place the coated avocado slices in a single layer in the air fryer basket.
5. Air fry at 375°F (190°C) for 8 minutes, or until golden and crispy, shaking halfway through.
6. Serve hot with your favorite dipping sauce.

NUTRITIONAL INFO (PER SERVING): Calories: 250 | Fat: 18g | Carbs: 20g | Protein: 5g

Kaloric Maxx Air Fryer Oven Functions Used: Air Fry

Tip: Use ripe but firm avocados to ensure the fries hold their shape.

Tip: For a tropical twist, serve with a side of sweet chili sauce or mango salsa.

AIR FRYER COCONUT SHRIMP

Prep: 15 mins | Cook: 10 mins | Serves: 4

INGREDIENTS:

- 1 lb (450g) large shrimp, peeled and deveined
- 1/2 cup (60g) all-purpose flour (plain flour)
- 2 large eggs, beaten
- 1 cup (100g) breadcrumbs
- 1 cup (100g) shredded coconut
- 1/2 teaspoon paprika
- Salt and pepper, to taste

INSTRUCTIONS:

1. Preheat your Kaloric Maxx Air Fryer Oven to 375°F (190°C) for 3 minutes.
2. Dredge each shrimp in flour, then dip in beaten eggs, and finally coat with breadcrumbs mixed with shredded coconut, paprika, salt, and pepper.
3. Place the coated shrimp in a single layer in the air fryer basket.
4. Air fry at 375°F (190°C) for 10 minutes, or until golden and crispy, shaking halfway through.
5. Serve hot with your favorite dipping sauce.

NUTRITIONAL INFO (PER SERVING): Calories: 320 | Fat: 12g | Carbs: 28g | Protein: 22g

Kaloric Maxx Air Fryer Oven Functions Used: Air Fry

AIR FRYER SPINACH ARTICHOKE DIP BITES

Prep: 20 mins | Cook: 8 mins | Serves: 4

INGREDIENTS:

- 1 cup (250g) spinach, cooked and drained
- 1 cup (250g) artichoke hearts, chopped
- 4 oz (115g) cream cheese, softened
- 1/2 cup (50g) grated Parmesan cheese
- 1/2 cup (50g) shredded mozzarella cheese
- 1/4 cup (25g) breadcrumbs
- 2 large eggs, beaten
- Salt and pepper, to taste

INSTRUCTIONS:

1. Preheat your Kaloric Maxx Air Fryer Oven to 375°F (190°C) for 3 minutes.
2. Mix spinach, artichoke hearts, cream cheese, Parmesan cheese, mozzarella cheese, salt, and pepper together in a bowl.
3. Form the mixture into bite-sized balls.
4. Dredge each ball in beaten eggs, then coat with breadcrumbs.
5. Place the coated bites in a single layer in the air fryer basket.
6. Air fry at 375°F (190°C) for 8 minutes, or until golden and crispy, shaking halfway through.
7. Serve hot.

NUTRITIONAL INFO (PER SERVING): Calories: 250 | Fat: 18g | Carbs: 10g | Protein: 10g

Kaloric Maxx Air Fryer Oven Functions Used: Air Fry

Tip: Freeze the bites for 15 minutes before air frying to help them hold their shape better.

AIR FRYER BACON-WRAPPED DATES

Prep: 10 mins | Cook: 10 mins | Serves: 4

INGREDIENTS:

- 16 dates, pitted
- 8 slices bacon, halved
- 16 almonds or pecans (optional)

INSTRUCTIONS:

1. Preheat your Kaloric Maxx Air Fryer Oven to 375°F (190°C) for 3 minutes.
2. Stuff each date with an almond or pecan, if using.
3. Wrap each date with a half slice of bacon, securing with a toothpick.
4. Place the bacon-wrapped dates in a single layer in the air fryer basket.
5. Air fry at 375°F (190°C) for 10 minutes, or until the bacon is crispy, shaking halfway through.
6. Serve hot.

NUTRITIONAL INFO (PER SERVING): Calories: 210 | Fat: 12g | Carbs: 22g | Protein: 6g

Tip: For a sweet and savory twist, drizzle the dates with a bit of honey before serving.

AIR FRYER ONION RINGS

Prep: 15 mins | Cook: 10 mins | Serves: 4

INGREDIENTS:

- 2 large onions, sliced into rings
- 1 cup (120g) all-purpose flour (plain flour)
- 2 large eggs, beaten
- 1 cup (100g) breadcrumbs
- 1/2 teaspoon paprika
- 1/2 teaspoon garlic powder
- Salt and pepper, to taste

INSTRUCTIONS:

1. Preheat your Kaloric Maxx Air Fryer Oven to 400°F (200°C) for 3 minutes.
2. Dredge each onion ring in flour, then dip in beaten eggs, and finally coat with breadcrumbs mixed with paprika, garlic powder, salt, and pepper.
3. Place the coated onion rings in a single layer in the air fryer basket.
4. Air fry at 400°F (200°C) for 10 minutes, or until golden and crispy, shaking halfway through.
5. Serve hot with your favorite dipping sauce.

NUTRITIONAL INFO (PER SERVING): Calories: 200 | Fat: 6g | Carbs: 34g | Protein: 5g

Kaloric Maxx Air Fryer Oven Functions Used: Air Fry

Tip: For even crispier onion rings, spray a light coat of cooking oil over them before air frying.

AIR FRYER STUFFED MUSHROOMS

Prep: 15 mins | Cook: 10 mins | Serves: 4

INGREDIENTS:

- 16 large white mushrooms, stems removed
- 4 oz (115g) cream cheese, softened
- 1/2 cup (50g) grated Parmesan cheese
- 1/4 cup (25g) breadcrumbs
- 2 cloves garlic, minced
- 2 tablespoons fresh parsley, chopped
- Salt and pepper, to taste

INSTRUCTIONS:

1. Preheat your Kaloric Maxx Air Fryer Oven to 375°F (190°C) for 3 minutes.
2. Mix cream cheese, Parmesan cheese, breadcrumbs, garlic, parsley, salt, and pepper together in a bowl.
3. Stuff each mushroom cap with the cheese mixture.
4. Place the stuffed mushrooms in a single layer in the air fryer basket.
5. Air fry at 375°F (190°C) for 10 minutes, or until the tops are golden and the cheese is bubbly.
6. Serve hot.

NUTRITIONAL INFO (PER SERVING): Calories: 160 | Fat: 12g | Carbs: 8g | Protein: 6g

Kaloric Maxx Air Fryer Oven Functions Used: Air Fry

Tip: Use large mushroom caps to make stuffing easier and to hold more filling.

AIR FRYER EMPANADAS

Prep: 20 mins | Cook: 12 mins | Serves: 4

INGREDIENTS:

- 1 package refrigerated pie crusts
- 1 cup (250g) cooked ground beef or chicken
- 1/2 cup (50g) shredded cheese
- 1/4 cup (30g) chopped bell pepper
- 1/4 cup (30g) chopped onion
- 1 teaspoon cumin
- 1/2 teaspoon paprika
- Salt and pepper, to taste

INSTRUCTIONS:

1. Preheat your Kaloric Maxx Air Fryer Oven to 375°F (190°C) for 3 minutes.
2. Roll out the pie crusts and cut into 4-inch circles.
3. Mix the cooked ground beef or chicken, shredded cheese, bell pepper, onion, cumin, paprika, salt, and pepper together in a bowl.
4. Place a tablespoon of filling in the center of each dough circle.
5. Fold the dough over to form a half-moon shape and press the edges to seal.
6. Place the empanadas in a single layer in the air fryer basket.
7. Air fry at 375°F (190°C) for 12 minutes, or until golden and crispy, shaking halfway through.
8. Serve hot.

NUTRITIONAL INFO (PER SERVING): Calories: 350 | Fat: 20g | Carbs: 30g | Protein: 10g

Kaloric Maxx Air Fryer Oven Functions Used: Air Fry

Tip: Use a fork to crimp the edges of the empanadas for a decorative and secure seal.

AIR FRYER PRETZEL BITES

Prep: 20 mins | Cook: 10 mins | Serves: 4

INGREDIENTS:

- 1 package refrigerated pizza dough
- 1/4 cup (60g) baking soda
- 1 egg, beaten
- Coarse salt, for sprinkling

INSTRUCTIONS:

1. Preheat your Kaloric Maxx Air Fryer Oven to 375°F (190°C) for 3 minutes.
2. Roll out the pizza dough and cut into 1-inch pieces to form bites.
3. Boil a pot of water and add the baking soda.
4. Drop the dough bites into the boiling water for 30 seconds, then remove and place on a paper towel to drain.
5. Brush the dough bites with beaten egg and sprinkle with coarse salt.
6. Place the pretzel bites in a single layer in the air fryer basket.
7. Air fry at 375°F (190°C) for 10 minutes, or until golden and crispy, shaking halfway through.
8. Serve hot with your favorite dipping sauce.

NUTRITIONAL INFO (PER SERVING): Calories: 200 | Fat: 5g | Carbs: 36g | Protein: 6g

Kaloric Maxx Air Fryer Oven Functions Used: Air Fry

Tip: Serve with a warm cheese sauce or mustard for a classic pretzel experience.

AIR FRYER CRISPY TOFU BITES

Prep: 10 mins | Cook: 15 mins | Serves: 4

INGREDIENTS:

- 1 block firm tofu, pressed and cubed
- 2 tablespoons soy sauce
- 1 tablespoon sesame oil
- 1/4 cup (30g) cornstarch
- 1/2 teaspoon garlic powder
- 1/2 teaspoon ginger powder
- Salt and pepper, to taste

INSTRUCTIONS:

1. Preheat your Kaloric Maxx Air Fryer Oven to 375°F (190°C) for 3 minutes.
2. Toss the tofu cubes with soy sauce and sesame oil in a bowl.
3. Mix the cornstarch, garlic powder, ginger powder, salt, and pepper together in another bowl.
4. Coat the tofu cubes in the cornstarch mixture.
5. Place the coated tofu cubes in a single layer in the air fryer basket.
6. Air fry at 375°F (190°C) for 15 minutes, or until golden and crispy, shaking halfway through.
7. Serve hot with your favorite dipping sauce.

NUTRITIONAL INFO (PER SERVING): Calories: 150 | Fat: 8g | Carbs: 10g | Protein: 10g

Kaloric Maxx Air Fryer Oven Functions Used: Air Fry

Tip: Serve with a soy-ginger dipping sauce for an extra burst of flavor.

BREAKFAST AND BRUNCH

AIR FRYER BREAKFAST FRITTATA

Prep: 10 mins | Cook: 15 mins | Serves: 4

INGREDIENTS:

- 6 large eggs
- 1/4 cup (60ml) milk
- 1/2 cup (50g) shredded cheddar cheese
- 1/2 cup (50g) chopped bell pepper
- 1/4 cup (25g) chopped onion
- 1/4 cup (25g) chopped spinach
- Salt and pepper, to taste

INSTRUCTIONS:

1. Preheat your Kaloric Maxx Air Fryer Oven to 350°F (180°C) using the Air Fry function.
2. Whisk together the eggs, milk, salt, and pepper in a large bowl.
3. Stir in the cheddar cheese, bell pepper, onion, and spinach.
4. Pour the mixture into a greased 7-inch round baking pan.
5. Place the pan in the air fryer basket.
6. Air fry at 350°F (180°C) for 15 minutes, or until the frittata is set and slightly golden on top.
7. Remove from the air fryer and let it cool for a few minutes before slicing.
8. Serve warm.

NUTRITIONAL INFO (PER SERVING): Calories: 150 | Fat: 10g | Carbs: 4g | Protein: 11g

Kaloric Maxx Air Fryer Oven Functions Used: Air Fry

Tip: Customize your frittata with your favorite veggies or cooked meats.

AIR FRYER FRENCH TOAST STICKS

Prep: 10 mins | Cook: 8 mins | Serves: 4

INGREDIENTS:

- 4 slices of thick bread
- 2 large eggs
- 1/2 cup (120ml) milk
- 1 teaspoon vanilla extract
- 1/2 teaspoon cinnamon
- 1 tablespoon sugar
- Cooking spray
- Maple syrup, for serving

INSTRUCTIONS:

1. Preheat your Kaloric Maxx Air Fryer Oven to 375°F (190°C) using the Air Fry function.
2. Cut each slice of bread into 3 sticks.
3. Whisk together the eggs, milk, vanilla extract, cinnamon, and sugar in a bowl.
4. Dip each bread stick into the egg mixture, ensuring they are well coated.
5. Spray the air fryer basket with cooking spray and place the bread sticks in a single layer.
6. Air fry at 375°F (190°C) for 8 minutes, flipping halfway through.
7. Serve warm with maple syrup.

NUTRITIONAL INFO (PER SERVING): Calories: 220 | Fat: 8g | Carbs: 28g | Protein: 7g

Kaloric Maxx Air Fryer Oven Functions Used: Air Fry

Tip: Dust with powdered sugar for an extra sweet touch.

AIR FRYER BACON AND EGG CUPS

Prep: 10 mins | Cook: 12 mins | Serves: 4

INGREDIENTS:

- 4 slices of bacon
- 4 large eggs
- 1/4 cup (25g) shredded cheese
- Salt and pepper, to taste
- Chopped chives, for garnish

INSTRUCTIONS:

1. Preheat your Kaloric Maxx Air Fryer Oven to 350°F (180°C) using the Air Fry function.
2. Line the inside of 4 muffin cups with a slice of bacon each, forming a cup shape.
3. Crack an egg into each bacon cup.
4. Sprinkle cheese, salt, and pepper over each egg.
5. Place the muffin cups in the air fryer basket.
6. Air fry at 350°F (180°C) for 12 minutes, or until the eggs are cooked to your liking.
7. Garnish with chopped chives and serve.

NUTRITIONAL INFO (PER SERVING): Calories: 200 | Fat: 15g | Carbs: 1g | Protein: 13g

Kaloric Maxx Air Fryer Oven Functions Used: Air Fry

Tip: Use silicone muffin cups for easy removal and cleanup.

AIR FRYER CINNAMON ROLLS

Prep: 15 mins | Cook: 12 mins | Serves: 8

INGREDIENTS:

- 1 can refrigerated cinnamon roll dough (8 rolls)
- Cooking spray

INSTRUCTIONS:

1. Preheat your Kaloric Maxx Air Fryer Oven to 360°F (180°C) using the Air Fry function.
2. Spray the air fryer basket with cooking spray.
3. Place the cinnamon rolls in a single layer in the air fryer basket.
4. Air fry at 360°F (180°C) for 12 minutes, or until golden brown.
5. Drizzle with the icing that comes with the rolls while they are still warm.
6. Serve immediately.

NUTRITIONAL INFO (PER SERVING): Calories: 190 | Fat: 6g | Carbs: 31g | Protein: 2g

Kaloric Maxx Air Fryer Oven Functions Used: Air Fry

Tip: For extra gooeyness, drizzle additional icing or melted butter over the warm rolls.

AIR FRYER BREAKFAST BURRITOS

Prep: 15 mins | Cook: 8 mins | Serves: 4

INGREDIENTS:

- 4 large flour tortillas
- 1 cup (100g) shredded cheddar cheese
- 1 cup (150g) cooked breakfast sausage, crumbled
- 1 cup (150g) scrambled eggs
- 1/2 cup (50g) salsa
- Cooking spray

INSTRUCTIONS:

1. Preheat your Kaloric Maxx Air Fryer Oven to 375°F (190°C) using the Air Fry function.
2. Lay out the tortillas and divide the cheese, sausage, scrambled eggs, and salsa evenly among them.
3. Roll up each tortilla, tucking in the ends to form burritos.
4. Spray the air fryer basket with cooking spray and place the burritos seam-side down in a single layer.
5. Air fry at 375°F (190°C) for 8 minutes, flipping halfway through.
6. Serve warm with extra salsa or sour cream.

NUTRITIONAL INFO (PER SERVING): Calories: 350 | Fat: 20g | Carbs: 30g | Protein: 15g

Kaloric Maxx Air Fryer Oven Functions Used: Air Fry

Tip: Secure the burritos with toothpicks if they tend to unroll during cooking.

AIR FRYER AVOCADO TOAST

Prep: 5 mins | Cook: 4 mins | Serves: 2

INGREDIENTS:

- 2 slices of bread
- 1 ripe avocado
- 1/2 teaspoon red pepper flakes
- 1 tablespoon olive oil
- Salt and pepper, to taste
- 1/4 lemon, juiced

INSTRUCTIONS:

1. Preheat your Kaloric Maxx Air Fryer Oven to 400°F (200°C) using the Air Fry function.
2. Brush the bread slices with olive oil on both sides.
3. Place the bread slices in the air fryer basket.
4. Air fry at 400°F (200°C) for 4 minutes, or until golden and crispy.
5. Mash the avocado in a bowl and mix with lemon juice, salt, and pepper.
6. Spread the avocado mixture over the toasted bread.
7. Sprinkle with red pepper flakes and serve immediately.

NUTRITIONAL INFO (PER SERVING): Calories: 250 | Fat: 18g | Carbs: 20g | Protein: 4g

Kaloric Maxx Air Fryer Oven Functions Used: Air Fry

Tip: Add a poached egg on top for extra protein.

AIR FRYER SAUSAGE PATTIES

Prep: 10 mins | Cook: 8 mins | Serves: 4

INGREDIENTS:

- 1 lb (450g) ground sausage
- 1/2 teaspoon garlic powder
- 1/2 teaspoon onion powder
- 1/4 teaspoon black pepper

INSTRUCTIONS:

1. Preheat your Kaloric Maxx Air Fryer Oven to 375°F (190°C) using the Air Fry function.
2. Mix the ground sausage, garlic powder, onion powder, and black pepper in a bowl.
3. Form the mixture into 8 patties.
4. Place the patties in a single layer in the air fryer basket.
5. Air fry at 375°F (190°C) for 8 minutes, flipping halfway through.
6. Serve hot.

NUTRITIONAL INFO (PER SERVING): Calories: 220 | Fat: 18g | Carbs: 1g | Protein: 13g

Kaloric Maxx Air Fryer Oven Functions Used: Air Fry

Tip: For a healthier option, use turkey sausage.

AIR FRYER BAGEL BITES

Prep: 10 mins | Cook: 8 mins | Serves: 4

INGREDIENTS:

- 4 mini bagels, halved
- 1/2 cup (125g) cream cheese
- 1/4 cup (25g) shredded cheddar cheese
- 1/4 cup (25g) chopped smoked salmon
- Fresh dill, for garnish

INSTRUCTIONS:

1. Preheat your Kaloric Maxx Air Fryer Oven to 375°F (190°C) using the Air Fry function.
2. Spread cream cheese evenly on each bagel half.
3. Top with shredded cheddar cheese and smoked salmon.
4. Place the bagel halves in a single layer in the air fryer basket.
5. Air fry at 375°F (190°C) for 8 minutes, or until the cheese is melted and bubbly.
6. Garnish with fresh dill and serve warm.

NUTRITIONAL INFO (PER SERVING): Calories: 180 | Fat: 9g | Carbs: 16g | Protein: 8g

Kaloric Maxx Air Fryer Oven Functions Used: Air Fry

Tip: Substitute the smoked salmon with your favorite bagel toppings.

AIR FRYER QUICHE

Prep: 15 mins | Cook: 15 mins | Serves: 4

INGREDIENTS:

- 1 pre-made pie crust
- 4 large eggs
- 1/2 cup (120ml) milk
- 1/2 cup (50g) shredded cheese
- 1/4 cup (25g) chopped ham
- 1/4 cup (25g) chopped spinach
- Salt and pepper, to taste

INSTRUCTIONS:

1. Preheat your Kaloric Maxx Air Fryer Oven to 350°F (180°C) using the Air Fry function.
2. Roll out the pie crust and fit it into a 7-inch pie dish.
3. Whisk together the eggs, milk, salt, and pepper.
4. Stir in the shredded cheese, ham, and spinach.
5. Pour the mixture into the pie crust.
6. Place the pie dish in the air fryer basket.
7. Air fry at 350°F (180°C) for 15 minutes, or until the quiche is set and slightly golden on top.
8. Let it cool for a few minutes before slicing and serving.

NUTRITIONAL INFO (PER SERVING): Calories: 250 | Fat: 18g | Carbs: 10g | Protein: 12g

Kaloric Maxx Air Fryer Oven Functions Used: Air Fry

Tip: Customize with your favorite quiche fillings.

AIR FRYER BREAKFAST POTATOES

Prep: 10 mins | Cook: 20 mins | Serves: 4

INGREDIENTS:

- 4 medium potatoes, diced
- 1 tablespoon olive oil
- 1 teaspoon paprika
- 1/2 teaspoon garlic powder
- Salt and pepper, to taste

INSTRUCTIONS:

1. Preheat your Kaloric Maxx Air Fryer Oven to 400°F (200°C) using the Air Fry function.
2. Toss the diced potatoes with olive oil, paprika, garlic powder, salt, and pepper in a bowl.
3. Place the potatoes in a single layer in the air fryer basket.
4. Air fry at 400°F (200°C) for 20 minutes, shaking the basket halfway through.
5. Serve hot.

NUTRITIONAL INFO (PER SERVING): Calories: 150 | Fat: 4g | Carbs: 26g | Protein: 3g

Kaloric Maxx Air Fryer Oven Functions Used: Air Fry | Tip: Add chopped onions and bell peppers for extra flavor.

AIR FRYER BANANA BREAD

Prep: 10 mins | Cook: 35 mins | Serves: 8

INGREDIENTS:

- 2 ripe bananas, mashed
- 1/3 cup (80ml) melted butter
- 1/2 cup (100g) sugar
- 1 large egg, beaten
- 1 teaspoon vanilla extract
- 1 teaspoon baking soda
- 1/4 teaspoon salt
- 1 1/2 cups (190g) all-purpose flour (plain flour)

INSTRUCTIONS:

1. Preheat your Kaloric Maxx Air Fryer Oven to 320°F (160°C) using the Bake function.
2. Mix the mashed bananas, melted butter, sugar, egg, and vanilla extract in a bowl.
3. Stir in the baking soda, salt, and flour until just combined.
4. Pour the batter into a greased 7-inch loaf pan.
5. Place the loaf pan in the air fryer basket.
6. Bake at 320°F (160°C) for 35 minutes, or until a toothpick inserted into the center comes out clean.
7. Let it cool before slicing and serving.

NUTRITIONAL INFO (PER SERVING): Calories: 220 | Fat: 8g | Carbs: 35g | Protein: 3g

Kaloric Maxx Air Fryer Oven Functions Used: Bake

Tip: Add chopped nuts or chocolate chips for a tasty variation.

AIR FRYER SCRAMBLED EGGS

Prep: 5 mins | Cook: 5 mins | Serves: 2

INGREDIENTS:

- 4 large eggs
- 1/4 cup (60ml) milk
- Salt and pepper, to taste
- 1 tablespoon butter

INSTRUCTIONS:

1. Preheat your Kaloric Maxx Air Fryer Oven to 300°F (150°C) using the Bake function.
2. Whisk together the eggs, milk, salt, and pepper in a bowl.
3. Pour the mixture into a greased baking dish.
4. Add small pats of butter on top of the egg mixture.
5. Place the baking dish in the air fryer basket.
6. Bake at 300°F (150°C) for 5 minutes, stirring halfway through.
7. Serve immediately.

NUTRITIONAL INFO (PER SERVING): Calories: 180 | Fat: 14g | Carbs: 2g | Protein: 11g

Kaloric Maxx Air Fryer Oven Functions Used: Bake

Tip: For creamier eggs, add a splash of heavy cream instead of milk.

AIR FRYER BLUEBERRY MUFFINS

Prep: 10 mins | Cook: 15 mins | Serves: 6

INGREDIENTS:

- 1 cup (125g) all-purpose flour (plain flour)
- 1/2 cup (100g) sugar
- 1/2 teaspoon baking powder
- 1/4 teaspoon baking soda
- 1/4 teaspoon salt
- 1/2 cup (120ml) milk
- 1/4 cup (60ml) vegetable oil
- 1 large egg
- 1 teaspoon vanilla extract
- 1 cup (150g) fresh blueberries

INSTRUCTIONS:

1. Preheat your Kaloric Maxx Air Fryer Oven to 350°F (180°C) using the Bake function.
2. Mix the flour, sugar, baking powder, baking soda, and salt in a bowl.
3. In another bowl, whisk together the milk, vegetable oil, egg, and vanilla extract.
4. Combine the wet and dry ingredients until just mixed.
5. Fold in the blueberries gently.
6. Divide the batter evenly among muffin cups.
7. Place the muffin cups in the air fryer basket.
8. Bake at 350°F (180°C) for 15 minutes, or until a toothpick inserted into the center comes out clean.
9. Let them cool before serving.

NUTRITIONAL INFO (PER SERVING): Calories: 180 | Fat: 8g | Carbs: 24g | Protein: 3g

Kaloric Maxx Air Fryer Oven Functions Used: Bake

Tip: Sprinkle a little sugar on top of the muffins before baking for a sweet crust.

AIR FRYER BREAKFAST PIZZA

Prep: 10 mins | Cook: 10 mins | Serves: 4

INGREDIENTS:

- 1 pre-made pizza crust
- 1/2 cup (125g) pizza sauce
- 1 cup (100g) shredded mozzarella cheese
- 4 large eggs
- 1/4 cup (25g) cooked breakfast sausage, crumbled
- 1/4 cup (25g) chopped bell pepper
- Salt and pepper, to taste

INSTRUCTIONS:

1. Preheat your Kaloric Maxx Air Fryer Oven to 400°F (200°C) using the Air Fry function.
2. Spread the pizza sauce evenly over the pizza crust.
3. Sprinkle the shredded mozzarella cheese on top.
4. Crack the eggs onto the pizza, spacing them out evenly.
5. Add the cooked breakfast sausage and chopped bell pepper.
6. Place the pizza in the air fryer basket.
7. Air fry at 400°F (200°C) for 10 minutes, or until the eggs are set and the cheese is melted and bubbly.
8. Season with salt and pepper and serve immediately.

NUTRITIONAL INFO (PER SERVING): Calories: 280 |

Fat: 14g | Carbs: 20g | Protein: 16g

Kaloric Maxx Air Fryer Oven Functions Used: Air Fry

Tip: Use a whole wheat crust for a healthier option.

AIR FRYER CROISSANTS

Prep: 10 mins | Cook: 10 mins | Serves: 4

INGREDIENTS:

- 1 can refrigerated crescent roll dough (8 rolls)
- 1/4 cup (60g) chocolate chips or jam (optional)

INSTRUCTIONS:

1. Preheat your Kaloric Maxx Air Fryer Oven to 350°F (180°C) using the Air Fry function.
2. Unroll the crescent roll dough and separate it into triangles.
3. Place a few chocolate chips or a spoonful of jam at the wide end of each triangle (if using).
4. Roll up each triangle, starting from the wide end, to form croissants.
5. Place the croissants in a single layer in the air fryer basket.
6. Air fry at 350°F (180°C) for 10 minutes, or until golden brown.
7. Serve warm.

NUTRITIONAL INFO (PER SERVING): Calories: 200 | Fat: 10g | Carbs: 25g | Protein: 3g

Kaloric Maxx Air Fryer Oven Functions Used: Air Fry

Tip: For an extra treat, drizzle melted chocolate over the warm croissants.

AIR FRYER FALAFEL

Prep: 15 mins | Cook: 15 mins | Serves: 4

INGREDIENTS:

- 2 cups (400g) canned chickpeas, drained and rinsed
- 1 small onion, finely chopped
- 2 cloves garlic, minced
- 1/4 cup (30g) fresh parsley, chopped
- 1/4 cup (30g) fresh cilantro, chopped
- 1 teaspoon cumin
- 1 teaspoon coriander
- 1/2 teaspoon baking powder
- 3 tablespoons flour (plain flour)
- Salt and pepper, to taste
- Cooking spray

INSTRUCTIONS:

1. Preheat your Kaloric Maxx Air Fryer Oven to 375°F (190°C) using the Air Fry function.
2. Blend the chickpeas, onion, garlic, parsley, cilantro, cumin, coriander, baking powder, and flour in a food processor until a coarse mixture forms.
3. Season with salt and pepper.
4. Form the mixture into small balls or patties.
5. Spray the air fryer basket with cooking spray and place the falafel balls in a single layer.
6. Air fry at 375°F (190°C) for 15 minutes, shaking halfway through.

NUTRITIONAL INFO (PER SERVING): Calories: 220 | Fat: 5g | Carbs: 34g | Protein: 10g

Kaloric Maxx Air Fryer Oven Functions Used: Air Fry

Tip: Serve with tahini sauce or in a pita with fresh veggies.

AIR FRYER VEGETABLE FRITTERS

Prep: 10 mins | Cook: 10 mins | Serves: 4

INGREDIENTS:

- 1 cup (150g) grated zucchini
- 1 cup (150g) grated carrot
- 1/2 cup (60g) chopped onion
- 1/2 cup (60g) flour (plain flour)
- 1/4 cup (30g) grated Parmesan cheese
- 1 large egg
- Salt and pepper, to taste
- Cooking spray

INSTRUCTIONS:

1. Preheat your Kaloric Maxx Air Fryer Oven to 375°F (190°C) using the Air Fry function.
2. Mix the zucchini, carrot, onion, flour, Parmesan cheese, egg, salt, and pepper in a bowl until well combined.
3. Form the mixture into small patties.
4. Spray the air fryer basket with cooking spray and place the fritters in a single layer.
5. Air fry at 375°F (190°C) for 10 minutes, flipping halfway through.

NUTRITIONAL INFO (PER SERVING): Calories: 120 | Fat: 5g | Carbs: 14g | Protein: 5g

Kaloric Maxx Air Fryer Oven Functions Used: Air Fry

Tip: Serve with a dollop of sour cream or yogurt.

AIR FRYER TOFU NUGGETS

Prep: 10 mins | Cook: 15 mins | Serves: 4

INGREDIENTS:

- 1 block (400g) firm tofu, pressed and cut into cubes
- 1/4 cup (60ml) soy sauce
- 1 tablespoon sesame oil
- 1 teaspoon garlic powder
- 1 teaspoon onion powder
- 1/2 cup (60g) breadcrumbs
- Cooking spray

INSTRUCTIONS:

1. Preheat your Kaloric Maxx Air Fryer Oven to 375°F (190°C) using the Air Fry function.
2. Marinate the tofu cubes in soy sauce, sesame oil, garlic powder, and onion powder for 10 minutes.
3. Coat the tofu cubes in breadcrumbs.
4. Spray the air fryer basket with cooking spray and place the tofu nuggets in a single layer.
5. Air fry at 375°F (190°C) for 15 minutes, shaking halfway through.

NUTRITIONAL INFO (PER SERVING): Calories: 180 | Fat: 8g | Carbs: 12g | Protein: 16g

Kaloric Maxx Air Fryer Oven Functions Used: Air Fry

Tip: Serve with your favorite dipping sauce.

AIR FRYER LENTIL PATTIES

Prep: 15 mins | Cook: 15 mins | Serves: 4

INGREDIENTS:

- 1 cup (200g) cooked lentils
- 1/2 cup (60g) breadcrumbs
- 1 small onion, finely chopped
- 2 cloves garlic, minced
- 1/4 cup (30g) chopped fresh parsley
- 1 teaspoon cumin
- Salt and pepper, to taste
- Cooking spray

INSTRUCTIONS:

1. Preheat your Kaloric Maxx Air Fryer Oven to 375°F (190°C) using the Air Fry function.
2. Combine the lentils, breadcrumbs, onion, garlic, parsley, cumin, salt, and pepper in a bowl.
3. Form the mixture into small patties.
4. Spray the air fryer basket with cooking spray and place the patties in a single layer.
5. Air fry at 375°F (190°C) for 15 minutes, flipping halfway through.

NUTRITIONAL INFO (PER SERVING): Calories: 200 | Fat: 4g | Carbs: 30g | Protein: 10g

Kaloric Maxx Air Fryer Oven Functions Used: Air Fry

Tip: Serve with a side salad or in a burger bun.

AIR FRYER STUFFED PORTOBELLO MUSHROOMS

Prep: 10 mins | Cook: 12 mins | Serves: 4

INGREDIENTS:

- 4 large Portobello mushrooms
- 1/2 cup (60g) breadcrumbs
- 1/4 cup (30g) grated Parmesan cheese
- 1/4 cup (30g) chopped spinach
- 2 cloves garlic, minced
- 2 tablespoons olive oil
- Salt and pepper, to taste

INSTRUCTIONS:

1. Preheat your Kaloric Maxx Air Fryer Oven to 350°F (180°C) using the Air Fry function.
2. Remove the stems and gills from the mushrooms.
3. Mix the breadcrumbs, Parmesan cheese, spinach, garlic, olive oil, salt, and pepper in a bowl.
4. Stuff the mushroom caps with the breadcrumb mixture.
5. Place the mushrooms in a single layer in the air fryer basket.
6. Air fry at 350°F (180°C) for 12 minutes, until the mushrooms are tender and the topping is golden.

NUTRITIONAL INFO (PER SERVING): Calories: 150 | Fat: 10g | Carbs: 12g | Protein: 4g

Kaloric Maxx Air Fryer Oven Functions Used: Air Fry

Tip: Serve as a main dish or a hearty side.

AIR FRYER EGGPLANT PARMESAN

Prep: 10 mins | Cook: 15 mins | Serves: 4

INGREDIENTS:

- 1 large eggplant, sliced into rounds
- 1 cup (120g) breadcrumbs
- 1/2 cup (60g) grated Parmesan cheese
- 1 teaspoon Italian seasoning
- 2 large eggs, beaten
- 1 cup (250ml) marinara sauce
- 1 cup (100g) shredded mozzarella cheese
- Cooking spray

INSTRUCTIONS:

1. Preheat your Kaloric Maxx Air Fryer Oven to 375°F (190°C) using the Air Fry function.
2. Combine the breadcrumbs, Parmesan cheese, and Italian seasoning in a bowl.
3. Dip each eggplant slice in beaten egg, then coat with the breadcrumb mixture.
4. Spray the air fryer basket with cooking spray and place the eggplant slices in a single layer.
5. Air fry at 375°F (190°C) for 15 minutes, flipping halfway through.
6. Top each slice with marinara sauce and shredded mozzarella cheese.
7. Air fry for an additional 3 minutes, until the cheese is melted.

NUTRITIONAL INFO (PER SERVING): Calories: 300 | Fat: 15g | Carbs: 30g | Protein: 14g

Kaloric Maxx Air Fryer Oven Functions Used: Air Fry

Tip: Serve with spaghetti for a complete meal.

AIR FRYER CAULIFLOWER WINGS

Prep: 10 mins | Cook: 20 mins | Serves: 4

INGREDIENTS:

- 1 head of cauliflower, cut into florets
- 1/2 cup (60g) flour (plain flour)
- 1/2 cup (120ml) water
- 1 teaspoon garlic powder
- 1 teaspoon paprika
- Salt and pepper, to taste
- 1/2 cup (125ml) buffalo sauce
- Cooking spray

INSTRUCTIONS:

1. Preheat your Kaloric Maxx Air Fryer Oven to 400°F (200°C) using the Air Fry function.
2. Mix the flour, water, garlic powder, paprika, salt, and pepper in a bowl to form a batter.
3. Dip each cauliflower floret in the batter, shaking off any excess.
4. Spray the air fryer basket with cooking spray and place the cauliflower in a single layer.
5. Air fry at 400°F (200°C) for 20 minutes, shaking halfway through.
6. Toss the cooked cauliflower in buffalo sauce and serve.

NUTRITIONAL INFO (PER SERVING): Calories: 100 | Fat: 3g | Carbs: 16g | Protein: 3g

Kaloric Maxx Air Fryer Oven Functions Used: Air Fry

Tip: Serve with ranch or blue cheese dressing.

AIR FRYER ROASTED BRUSSELS SPROUTS

Prep: 5 mins | Cook: 15 mins | Serves: 4

INGREDIENTS:

- 1 lb (450g) Brussels sprouts, trimmed and halved
- 2 tablespoons olive oil
- Salt and pepper, to taste
- 1 tablespoon balsamic vinegar (optional)

INSTRUCTIONS:

1. Preheat your Kaloric Maxx Air Fryer Oven to 375°F (190°C) using the Air Fry function.
2. Toss the Brussels sprouts with olive oil, salt, and pepper.
3. Place the Brussels sprouts in a single layer in the air fryer basket.
4. Air fry at 375°F (190°C) for 15 minutes, shaking halfway through.
5. Drizzle with balsamic vinegar before serving, if desired.

NUTRITIONAL INFO (PER SERVING): Calories: 110 | Fat: 7g | Carbs: 10g | Protein: 3g

Kaloric Maxx Air Fryer Oven Functions Used: Air Fry

Tip: Add a sprinkle of Parmesan cheese for extra flavor.

AIR FRYER BAKED POTATOES

Prep: 5 mins | Cook: 35 mins | Serves: 4

INGREDIENTS:

- 4 medium russet potatoes
- 2 tablespoons olive oil
- Salt and pepper, to taste

INSTRUCTIONS:

1. Preheat your Kaloric Maxx Air Fryer Oven to 400°F (200°C) using the Air Fry function.
2. Prick each potato with a fork several times.
3. Rub the potatoes with olive oil, salt, and pepper.
4. Place the potatoes in a single layer in the air fryer basket.
5. Air fry at 400°F (200°C) for 35 minutes, turning halfway through, until the potatoes are tender.

NUTRITIONAL INFO (PER SERVING): Calories: 200 | Fat: 7g | Carbs: 36g | Protein: 4g

Kaloric Maxx Air Fryer Oven Functions Used: Air Fry

Tip: Serve with your favorite toppings like sour cream, cheese, and chives.

AIR FRYER VEGGIE BURGERS

Prep: 15 mins | Cook: 15 mins | Serves: 4

INGREDIENTS:

- 1 can (400g) black beans, drained and rinsed
- 1/2 cup (60g) breadcrumbs
- 1/4 cup (30g) finely chopped onion
- 1/4 cup (30g) finely chopped bell pepper
- 1 clove garlic, minced
- 1 teaspoon cumin
- Salt and pepper, to taste
- Cooking spray

INSTRUCTIONS:

1. Preheat your Kaloric Maxx Air Fryer Oven to 375°F (190°C) using the Air Fry function.
2. Mash the black beans in a bowl.
3. Add the breadcrumbs, onion, bell pepper, garlic, cumin, salt, and pepper. Mix until well combined.
4. Form the mixture into patties.
5. Spray the air fryer basket with cooking spray and place the patties in a single layer.
6. Air fry at 375°F (190°C) for 15 minutes, flipping halfway through.

NUTRITIONAL INFO (PER SERVING): Calories: 180 | Fat: 4g | Carbs: 30g | Protein: 6g

Kaloric Maxx Air Fryer Oven Functions Used: Air Fry

Tip: Serve on a bun with your favorite burger toppings.

AIR FRYER JACKFRUIT TACOS

Prep: 15 mins | Cook: 10 mins | Serves: 4

INGREDIENTS:

- 1 can (400g) young green jackfruit, drained and shredded
- 1/2 cup (125ml) barbecue sauce
- 1 teaspoon smoked paprika
- 1 teaspoon garlic powder
- Salt and pepper, to taste
- 8 small tortillas
- Toppings: shredded lettuce, diced tomatoes, avocado, cilantro

INSTRUCTIONS:

1. Preheat your Kaloric Maxx Air Fryer Oven to 375°F (190°C) using the Air Fry function.
2. Mix the shredded jackfruit with barbecue sauce, smoked paprika, garlic powder, salt, and pepper.
3. Spread the jackfruit mixture in the air fryer basket.
4. Air fry at 375°F (190°C) for 10 minutes, shaking halfway through.
5. Serve the jackfruit in tortillas with your favorite toppings.

NUTRITIONAL INFO (PER SERVING): Calories: 220 | Fat: 4g | Carbs: 42g | Protein: 3g

Kaloric Maxx Air Fryer Oven Functions Used: Air Fry

Tip: Add a squeeze of lime for extra flavor.

AIR FRYER CRISPY TOFU BITES

Prep: 10 mins | Cook: 15 mins | Serves: 4

INGREDIENTS:

- 1 block (400g) firm tofu, pressed and cubed
- 1/4 cup (60ml) soy sauce
- 1 tablespoon sesame oil
- 1/2 cup (60g) cornstarch
- Cooking spray

INSTRUCTIONS:

1. Preheat your Kaloric Maxx Air Fryer Oven to 375°F (190°C) using the Air Fry function.
2. Marinate the tofu cubes in soy sauce and sesame oil for 10 minutes.
3. Coat the tofu cubes in cornstarch.
4. Spray the air fryer basket with cooking spray and place the tofu in a single layer.
5. Air fry at 375°F (190°C) for 15 minutes, shaking halfway through.

NUTRITIONAL INFO (PER SERVING): Calories: 180 | Fat: 9g | Carbs: 10g | Protein: 14g

Kaloric Maxx Air Fryer Oven Functions Used: Air Fry

Tip: Serve with a sweet chili dipping sauce.

AIR FRYER CHICKPEA FRIES

Prep: 10 mins | Cook: 15 mins | Serves: 4

INGREDIENTS:

- 1 can (400g) chickpeas, drained and rinsed
- 1/4 cup (30g) flour (plain flour)
- 1 teaspoon cumin
- 1 teaspoon paprika
- Salt and pepper, to taste
- Cooking spray

INSTRUCTIONS:

1. Preheat your Kaloric Maxx Air Fryer Oven to 375°F (190°C) using the Air Fry function.
2. Mash the chickpeas in a bowl.
3. Add the flour, cumin, paprika, salt, and pepper. Mix until well combined.
4. Form the mixture into fry shapes.
5. Spray the air fryer basket with cooking spray and place the fries in a single layer.
6. Air fry at 375°F (190°C) for 15 minutes, shaking halfway through.

NUTRITIONAL INFO (PER SERVING): Calories: 150 | Fat: 4g | Carbs: 24g | Protein: 5g

Kaloric Maxx Air Fryer Oven Functions Used: Air Fry

Tip: Serve with ketchup or aioli.

AIR FRYER ROASTED VEGETABLES

Prep: 10 mins | Cook: 20 mins | Serves: 4

INGREDIENTS:

- 1 cup (150g) chopped bell peppers
- 1 cup (150g) chopped zucchini
- 1 cup (150g) chopped carrots
- 1 cup (150g) chopped broccoli
- 2 tablespoons olive oil
- 1 teaspoon Italian seasoning
- Salt and pepper, to taste

INSTRUCTIONS:

1. Preheat your Kaloric Maxx Air Fryer Oven to 375°F (190°C) using the Air Fry function.
2. Toss all the vegetables with olive oil, Italian seasoning, salt, and pepper.
3. Place the vegetables in a single layer in the air fryer basket.
4. Air fry at 375°F (190°C) for 20 minutes, shaking halfway through.

NUTRITIONAL INFO (PER SERVING): Calories: 110 | Fat: 7g | Carbs: 10g | Protein: 2g

Kaloric Maxx Air Fryer Oven Functions Used: Air Fry

Tip: Add a squeeze of lemon juice for a fresh finish.

AIR FRYER VEGGIE KABOBS

Prep: 15 mins | Cook: 10 mins | Serves: 4

INGREDIENTS:

- 1 cup (150g) cherry tomatoes
- 1 cup (150g) bell peppers, chopped
- 1 cup (150g) zucchini, sliced
- 1 cup (150g) red onion, chopped
- 2 tablespoons olive oil
- 1 teaspoon garlic powder
- 1 teaspoon dried oregano
- Salt and pepper, to taste

INSTRUCTIONS:

1. Preheat your Kaloric Maxx Air Fryer Oven to 375°F (190°C) using the Air Fry function.
2. Thread the vegetables onto skewers.
3. Mix the olive oil, garlic powder, oregano, salt, and pepper in a small bowl.
4. Brush the vegetable skewers with the oil mixture.
5. Place the skewers in a single layer in the air fryer basket.
6. Air fry at 375°F (190°C) for 10 minutes, turning halfway through.

NUTRITIONAL INFO (PER SERVING): Calories: 120 | Fat: 7g | Carbs: 12g | Protein: 2g

Kaloric Maxx Air Fryer Oven Functions Used: Air Fry

Tip: Serve with a side of hummus or tzatziki.

POULTRY DISHES

AIR FRYER WHOLE ROASTED CHICKEN

Prep: 10 mins | Cook: 1 hour 15 mins | Serves: 6

INGREDIENTS:

- 1 whole chicken (4-5 lbs / 1.8-2.3 kg)
- 2 tablespoons olive oil
- 1 teaspoon garlic powder
- 1 teaspoon paprika
- 1 teaspoon dried thyme
- Salt and pepper, to taste
- 1 lemon, halved
- 4 garlic cloves

INSTRUCTIONS:

1. Preheat your Kaloric Maxx Air Fryer Oven to 375°F (190°C) using the Air Roast function.
2. Pat dry the chicken with paper towels. Rub it all over with olive oil.
3. Mix the garlic powder, paprika, thyme, salt, and pepper. Sprinkle evenly over the chicken.
4. Stuff the cavity with lemon halves and garlic cloves.
5. Place the chicken breast-side down in the air fryer basket.
6. Air roast at 375°F (190°C) for 45 minutes. Flip the chicken and cook for an additional 30 minutes, or until the internal temperature reaches 165°F (75°C).

NUTRITIONAL INFO (PER SERVING): Calories: 450 | Fat: 26g | Carbs: 1g | Protein: 49g

Kaloric Maxx Air Fryer Oven Functions Used: Air Roast

Tip: Let the chicken rest for 10 minutes before carving to keep it juicy.

AIR FRYER CHICKEN TENDERS

Prep: 10 mins | Cook: 15 mins | Serves: 4

INGREDIENTS:

- 1 lb (450g) chicken tenders
- 1 cup (120g) breadcrumbs
- 1/2 cup (60g) grated Parmesan cheese
- 1 teaspoon garlic powder
- 1 teaspoon paprika
- Salt and pepper, to taste
- 2 eggs, beaten
- Cooking spray

INSTRUCTIONS:

1. Preheat your Kaloric Maxx Air Fryer Oven to 400°F (200°C) using the Air Fry function.
2. Combine breadcrumbs, Parmesan, garlic powder, paprika, salt, and pepper in a bowl.
3. Dip each chicken tender in beaten eggs, then coat with the breadcrumb mixture.
4. Spray the air fryer basket with cooking spray and place the tenders in a single layer.
5. Air fry at 400°F (200°C) for 15 minutes, flipping halfway through.

NUTRITIONAL INFO (PER SERVING): Calories: 310 | Fat: 10g | Carbs: 20g | Protein: 32g

Kaloric Maxx Air Fryer Oven Functions Used: Air Fry

Tip: Serve with your favorite dipping sauce.

AIR FRYER CHICKEN PARMESAN

Prep: 10 mins | Cook: 15 mins | Serves: 4

INGREDIENTS:

- 4 boneless, skinless chicken breasts
- 1 cup (120g) breadcrumbs
- 1/2 cup (60g) grated Parmesan cheese
- 1 teaspoon Italian seasoning
- 1/2 teaspoon garlic powder
- Salt and pepper, to taste
- 1 egg, beaten
- 1 cup (240ml) marinara sauce
- 1 cup (100g) shredded mozzarella cheese
- Cooking spray

INSTRUCTIONS:

1. Preheat your Kaloric Maxx Air Fryer Oven to 380°F (190°C) using the Air Fry function.
2. Combine breadcrumbs, Parmesan, Italian seasoning, garlic powder, salt, and pepper in a bowl.
3. Dip each chicken breast in beaten egg, then coat with the breadcrumb mixture.
4. Spray the air fryer basket with cooking spray and place the chicken breasts in a single layer.
5. Air fry at 380°F (190°C) for 12 minutes, flipping halfway through.

6. Top each chicken breast with marinara sauce and mozzarella cheese. Air fry for an additional 3 minutes, or until the cheese is melted.

NUTRITIONAL INFO (PER SERVING): Calories: 400 | Fat: 15g | Carbs: 25g | Protein: 40g

Kaloric Maxx Air Fryer Oven Functions Used: Air Fry

Tip: Serve with pasta or a side salad.

AIR FRYER CHICKEN FAJITAS

Prep: 10 mins | Cook: 15 mins | Serves: 4

INGREDIENTS:

- 1 lb (450g) boneless, skinless chicken breasts, sliced
- 1 red bell pepper, sliced
- 1 green bell pepper, sliced
- 1 yellow bell pepper, sliced
- 1 onion, sliced
- 2 tablespoons olive oil
- 1 teaspoon chili powder
- 1 teaspoon cumin
- 1/2 teaspoon garlic powder
- 1/2 teaspoon paprika
- Salt and pepper, to taste
- Tortillas and toppings of your choice

INSTRUCTIONS:

1. Preheat your Kaloric Maxx Air Fryer Oven to 400°F (200°C) using the Air Fry function.
2. Combine chicken, bell peppers, onion, olive oil, chili powder, cumin, garlic powder, paprika, salt, and pepper in a bowl. Mix well.

3. Place the mixture in the air fryer basket in a single layer.
4. Air fry at 400°F (200°C) for 15 minutes, shaking halfway through.

NUTRITIONAL INFO (PER SERVING): Calories: 290 | Fat: 12g | Carbs: 10g | Protein: 34g

Kaloric Maxx Air Fryer Oven Functions Used: Air Fry

Tip: Serve with warm tortillas, sour cream, and salsa.

4. Air fry at 375°F (190°C) for 15 minutes, shaking halfway through.
5. Garnish with sesame seeds and green onions before serving.

NUTRITIONAL INFO (PER SERVING): Calories: 310 | Fat: 14g | Carbs: 20g | Protein: 27g

Kaloric Maxx Air Fryer Oven Functions Used: Air Fry

Tip: Serve with steamed rice and vegetables.

AIR FRYER TERIYAKI CHICKEN

Prep: 10 mins | Cook: 15 mins | Serves: 4

INGREDIENTS:

- 1 lb (450g) boneless, skinless chicken thighs, cut into pieces
- 1/4 cup (60ml) soy sauce
- 1/4 cup (60ml) teriyaki sauce
- 2 tablespoons honey
- 1 tablespoon sesame oil
- 1 teaspoon garlic powder
- 1 teaspoon ginger powder
- Sesame seeds and green onions for garnish

INSTRUCTIONS:

1. Preheat your Kaloric Maxx Air Fryer Oven to 375°F (190°C) using the Air Fry function.
2. Combine soy sauce, teriyaki sauce, honey, sesame oil, garlic powder, and ginger powder in a bowl. Add chicken pieces and marinate for 10 minutes.
3. Place the chicken pieces in the air fryer basket in a single layer.

AIR FRYER CHICKEN TIKKA MASALA

Prep: 20 mins | Cook: 25 mins | Serves: 4

INGREDIENTS:

- 1 lb (450g) boneless, skinless chicken breasts, cubed
- 1/2 cup (125ml) plain yogurt
- 2 tablespoons lemon juice
- 1 tablespoon ginger paste
- 1 tablespoon garlic paste
- 1 teaspoon turmeric
- 1 teaspoon garam masala
- 1 teaspoon cumin
- 1/2 teaspoon chili powder
- Salt, to taste
- 1 cup (240ml) tomato sauce
- 1/2 cup (120ml) heavy cream
- 1 tablespoon butter
- Fresh cilantro for garnish

INSTRUCTIONS:

1. Preheat your Kaloric Maxx Air Fryer Oven to 375°F (190°C) using the Air Fry function.
2. Mix yogurt, lemon juice, ginger paste, garlic paste, turmeric, garam masala, cumin, chili powder, and salt in a bowl. Add chicken cubes and marinate for 20 minutes.
3. Place the chicken cubes in the air fryer basket in a single layer.
4. Air fry at 375°F (190°C) for 15 minutes, shaking halfway through.
5. In a pan, heat butter, add tomato sauce, and bring to a simmer. Stir in heavy cream and cook for 5 minutes.
6. Add the cooked chicken to the sauce and simmer for another 5 minutes.
7. Garnish with fresh cilantro before serving.

NUTRITIONAL INFO (PER SERVING): Calories: 370 | Fat: 21g | Carbs: 13g | Protein

AIR FRYER LEMON GARLIC CHICKEN

Prep: 10 mins | Cook: 20 mins | Serves: 4

INGREDIENTS:

- 4 boneless, skinless chicken breasts
- 1/4 cup (60ml) olive oil
- 3 cloves garlic, minced
- 1 lemon, juiced and zested
- 1 teaspoon dried oregano
- 1/2 teaspoon salt
- 1/4 teaspoon black pepper
- Fresh parsley for garnish

INSTRUCTIONS:

1. Preheat your Kaloric Maxx Air Fryer Oven to 375°F (190°C) using the Air Fry function.
2. In a bowl, combine olive oil, garlic, lemon juice and zest, oregano, salt, and pepper.
3. Place chicken breasts in the bowl and coat evenly with the marinade.
4. Let marinate for 10 minutes.
5. Place the chicken breasts in a single layer in the air fryer basket.
6. Air fry at 375°F (190°C) for 20 minutes, flipping halfway through, until the internal temperature reaches 165°F (75°C).
7. Garnish with fresh parsley before serving.

NUTRITIONAL INFO (PER SERVING): Calories: 280 | Fat: 16g | Carbs: 2g | Protein: 29g

Kaloric Maxx Air Fryer Oven Functions Used: Air Fry

Tip: Serve with roasted vegetables or a fresh salad.

AIR FRYER BUFFALO CHICKEN WINGS

Prep: 10 mins | Cook: 25 mins | Serves: 4

INGREDIENTS:

- 2 lbs (900g) chicken wings
- 2 tablespoons olive oil
- 1 teaspoon garlic powder
- 1 teaspoon paprika
- 1/2 teaspoon salt
- 1/4 teaspoon black pepper
- 1/2 cup (120ml) buffalo sauce
- 2 tablespoons butter, melted
- Celery sticks and blue cheese dressing for serving

INSTRUCTIONS:

1. Preheat your Kaloric Maxx Air Fryer Oven to 400°F (200°C) using the Air Fry function.
2. In a bowl, toss the chicken wings with olive oil, garlic powder, paprika, salt, and pepper.
3. Place the wings in a single layer in the air fryer basket.
4. Air fry at 400°F (200°C) for 25 minutes, shaking the basket halfway through.
5. In another bowl, mix buffalo sauce and melted butter.
6. Toss the cooked wings in the buffalo sauce mixture.
7. Serve with celery sticks and blue cheese dressing.

NUTRITIONAL INFO (PER SERVING): Calories: 360 | Fat: 24g | Carbs: 2g | Protein: 31g

Kaloric Maxx Air Fryer Oven Functions Used: Air Fry

Tip: For extra crispy wings, air fry for an additional 5 minutes.

AIR FRYER CHICKEN LETTUCE WRAPS

Prep: 15 mins | Cook: 12 mins | Serves: 4

INGREDIENTS:

- 1 lb (450g) ground chicken
- 1 tablespoon olive oil
- 2 cloves garlic, minced
- 1 small onion, diced
- 1/2 cup (75g) water chestnuts, diced
- 1/4 cup (60ml) hoisin sauce
- 2 tablespoons soy sauce
- 1 tablespoon rice vinegar
- 1 teaspoon sesame oil
- Lettuce leaves for serving
- Green onions and sesame seeds for garnish

INSTRUCTIONS:

1. Preheat your Kaloric Maxx Air Fryer Oven to 380°F (190°C) using the Air Fry function.
2. Heat olive oil in a skillet over medium heat. Add garlic and onion, and cook until fragrant, about 3 minutes.
3. Add ground chicken and cook until browned, about 5 minutes.
4. Stir in water chestnuts, hoisin sauce, soy sauce, rice vinegar, and sesame oil. Cook for another 2 minutes.
5. Transfer the mixture to the air fryer basket.
6. Air fry at 380°F (190°C) for 12 minutes, shaking halfway through.
7. Serve the chicken mixture in lettuce leaves, garnished with green onions and sesame seeds.

NUTRITIONAL INFO (PER SERVING): Calories: 280 | Fat: 14g | Carbs: 12g | Protein: 24g

Kaloric Maxx Air Fryer Oven Functions Used: Air Fry

Tip: Add a splash of sriracha for a spicy kick.

AIR FRYER CHICKEN CORDON BLEU

Prep: 15 mins | Cook: 20 mins | Serves: 4

INGREDIENTS:

- 4 boneless, skinless chicken breasts
- 4 slices of ham
- 4 slices of Swiss cheese
- 1 cup (120g) breadcrumbs
- 1/2 cup (60g) grated Parmesan cheese
- 1 teaspoon garlic powder
- 1 teaspoon paprika
- 2 eggs, beaten
- Cooking spray

INSTRUCTIONS:

1. Preheat your Kaloric Maxx Air Fryer Oven to 375°F (190°C) using the Air Fry function.
2. Butterfly the chicken breasts and place a slice of ham and cheese inside each.
3. Secure with toothpicks.
4. Combine breadcrumbs, Parmesan, garlic powder, and paprika in a bowl.
5. Dip each stuffed chicken breast in beaten eggs, then coat with the breadcrumb mixture.
6. Spray the air fryer basket with cooking spray and place the chicken breasts in a single layer.
7. Air fry at 375°F (190°C) for 20 minutes, flipping halfway through, until the internal temperature reaches 165°F (75°C).

NUTRITIONAL INFO (PER SERVING): Calories: 420 | Fat: 18g | Carbs: 20g | Protein: 46g

Kaloric Maxx Air Fryer Oven Functions Used: Air Fry

Tip: Serve with steamed vegetables and mashed potatoes.

AIR FRYER CHICKEN KABOBS

Prep: 15 mins | Cook: 15 mins | Serves: 4

INGREDIENTS:

- 1 lb (450g) boneless, skinless chicken breasts, cut into cubes
- 1 red bell pepper, cut into pieces
- 1 green bell pepper, cut into pieces
- 1 red onion, cut into pieces
- 2 tablespoons olive oil
- 1 teaspoon garlic powder
- 1 teaspoon paprika
- 1 teaspoon dried oregano
- Salt and pepper, to taste
- Wooden or metal skewers

INSTRUCTIONS:

1. Preheat your Kaloric Maxx Air Fryer Oven to 380°F (190°C) using the Air Fry function.
2. In a bowl, combine olive oil, garlic powder, paprika, oregano, salt, and pepper.
3. Thread chicken and vegetables onto skewers.
4. Brush the skewers with the olive oil mixture.
5. Place the skewers in the air fryer basket in a single layer.
6. Air fry at 380°F (190°C) for 15 minutes, turning halfway through.

NUTRITIONAL INFO (PER SERVING): Calories: 220 | Fat: 11g | Carbs: 6g | Protein: 23g

Kaloric Maxx Air Fryer Oven Functions Used: Air Fry

Tip: Serve with a side of tzatziki sauce.

AIR FRYER CHICKEN POT PIE

Prep: 15 mins | Cook: 25 mins | Serves: 4

INGREDIENTS:

- 1 lb (450g) boneless, skinless chicken breasts, cubed
- 1 cup (150g) frozen peas and carrots
- 1/2 cup (60g) frozen corn
- 1/2 cup (120ml) chicken broth
- 1/2 cup (120ml) heavy cream
- 1 tablespoon butter
- 1 teaspoon garlic powder
- 1 teaspoon onion powder
- Salt and pepper, to taste
- 1 sheet puff pastry, thawed

INSTRUCTIONS:

1. Preheat your Kaloric Maxx Air Fryer Oven to 375°F (190°C) using the Air Fry function.
2. In a pan, melt butter over medium heat. Add chicken and cook until browned, about 5 minutes.
3. Stir in peas, carrots, corn, chicken broth, heavy cream, garlic powder, onion powder, salt, and pepper. Cook until the mixture thickens, about 5 minutes.
4. Pour the mixture into a baking dish that fits your air fryer.
5. Cut the puff pastry to fit the top of the dish and place it over the filling.

6. Air fry at 375°F (190°C) for 25 minutes, or until the pastry is golden brown and puffed.

NUTRITIONAL INFO (PER SERVING): Calories: 420 | Fat: 25g | Carbs: 25g | Protein: 20g

Kaloric Maxx Air Fryer Oven Functions Used: Air Fry

Tip: Let cool for a few minutes before serving to avoid burns from the hot filling.

AIR FRYER CHICKEN ENCHILADAS

Prep: 15 mins | Cook: 20 mins | Serves: 4

INGREDIENTS:

- 2 cups (300g) cooked, shredded chicken
- 1 cup (240ml) enchilada sauce
- 1 cup (100g) shredded cheddar cheese
- 1/2 cup (75g) diced green chilies
- 8 small flour tortillas
- Cooking spray
- Fresh cilantro for garnish

INSTRUCTIONS:

1. Preheat your Kaloric Maxx Air Fryer Oven to 375°F (190°C) using the Air Fry function.
2. In a bowl, combine shredded chicken, 1/2 cup (120ml) enchilada sauce, cheese, and green chilies.
3. Spoon the mixture into tortillas, roll them up, and place them seam-side down in a baking dish that fits your air fryer.
4. Pour the remaining enchilada sauce over the top.

5. Spray with cooking spray and air fry at 375°F (190°C) for 20 minutes, until the cheese is melted and bubbly.
6. Garnish with fresh cilantro before serving.

NUTRITIONAL INFO (PER SERVING): Calories: 340 | Fat: 18g | Carbs: 24g | Protein: 21g

Kaloric Maxx Air Fryer Oven Functions Used: Air Fry

Tip: Serve with a side of Mexican rice and beans.

AIR FRYER CHICKEN DRUMSTICKS

Prep: 10 mins | Cook: 25 mins | Serves: 4

INGREDIENTS:

- 8 chicken drumsticks
- 2 tablespoons olive oil
- 1 teaspoon garlic powder
- 1 teaspoon paprika
- 1/2 teaspoon dried thyme
- Salt and pepper, to taste

INSTRUCTIONS:

1. Preheat your Kaloric Maxx Air Fryer Oven to 400°F (200°C) using the Air Fry function.
2. In a bowl, toss the drumsticks with olive oil, garlic powder, paprika, thyme, salt, and pepper.
3. Place the drumsticks in the air fryer basket in a single layer.
4. Air fry at 400°F (200°C) for 25 minutes, flipping halfway through, until the internal temperature reaches 165°F (75°C).

NUTRITIONAL INFO (PER SERVING): Calories: 290 | Fat: 18g | Carbs: 1g | Protein: 29g

Kaloric Maxx Air Fryer Oven Functions Used: Air Fry

Tip: Pair with a simple green salad for a balanced meal.

AIR FRYER ROTISSERIE CHICKEN

Prep: 10 mins | Cook: 1 hour 15 mins | Serves: 6

INGREDIENTS:

- 1 whole chicken (4-5 lbs / 1.8-2.3 kg)
- 2 tablespoons olive oil
- 1 teaspoon garlic powder
- 1 teaspoon paprika
- 1 teaspoon dried thyme
- Salt and pepper, to taste
- 1 lemon, halved
- 4 garlic cloves

INSTRUCTIONS:

1. Preheat your Kaloric Maxx Air Fryer Oven to 375°F (190°C) using the Rotisserie function.
2. Pat dry the chicken with paper towels. Rub it all over with olive oil.
3. Mix the garlic powder, paprika, thyme, salt, and pepper. Sprinkle evenly over the chicken.
4. Stuff the cavity with lemon halves and garlic cloves.
5. Insert the rotisserie spit through the chicken and secure it.
6. Place the chicken in the air fryer and set the Rotisserie function for 1 hour and 15 minutes, or until the internal temperature reaches 165°F (75°C).

NUTRITIONAL INFO (PER SERVING): Calories: 450 | Fat: 26g | Carbs: 1g | Protein: 49g

Kaloric Maxx Air Fryer Oven Functions Used: Rotisserie

Tip: Let the chicken rest for 10 minutes before carving to keep it juicy.

BEEF AND PORK DISHES

AIR FRYER STEAK FRITES

Prep: 15 mins | Cook: 20 mins | Serves: 2

INGREDIENTS:

- 2 beef sirloin steaks (8 oz each) / 2 beef sirloin steaks (225g each)
- 2 large potatoes, cut into fries / 2 large potatoes, cut into chips
- 2 tablespoons olive oil / 2 tablespoons olive oil
- Salt and pepper, to taste / Salt and pepper, to taste
- Fresh parsley, chopped, for garnish / Fresh parsley, chopped, for garnish

INSTRUCTIONS:

1. Preheat your Kaloric Maxx Air Fryer Oven to 400°F (200°C) using the Air Fry function.
2. Toss the potato fries with olive oil, salt, and pepper in a bowl.
3. Place the seasoned fries in the air fryer basket in a single layer.
4. Air fry at 400°F (200°C) for 15-20 minutes, shaking the basket halfway through, until golden and crispy.
5. While the fries cook, season the steaks with salt and pepper.
6. Place the steaks in the air fryer basket.
7. Air fry at 400°F (200°C) for 10-12 minutes for medium-rare, flipping halfway through.
8. Let the steaks rest for a few minutes before serving.
9. Serve the steak with the crispy fries, garnished with chopped parsley.

NUTRITIONAL INFO (PER SERVING): Calories: 550 | Fat: 25g | Carbs: 50g | Protein: 32g

Kaloric Maxx Air Fryer Oven Functions Used: Air Fry

Tip: For added flavor, sprinkle the fries with grated Parmesan cheese before serving.

AIR FRYER MEATBALLS

Prep: 20 mins | Cook: 15 mins | Serves: 4

INGREDIENTS:

- 1 lb (450g) ground beef / 450g minced beef
- 1/2 cup (50g) breadcrumbs / 50g breadcrumbs
- 1/4 cup (25g) grated Parmesan cheese / 25g grated Parmesan cheese
- 1 egg, lightly beaten / 1 egg, lightly beaten
- 2 cloves garlic, minced / 2 cloves garlic, minced
- 1 teaspoon dried oregano / 1 teaspoon dried oregano
- 1/2 teaspoon salt / 1/2 teaspoon salt
- 1/4 teaspoon black pepper / 1/4 teaspoon black pepper
- Marinara sauce, for serving / Marinara sauce, for serving

INSTRUCTIONS:

1. Preheat your Kaloric Maxx Air Fryer Oven to 375°F (190°C) using the Air Fry function.
2. In a bowl, combine ground beef, breadcrumbs, Parmesan cheese, egg, garlic, oregano, salt, and pepper.
3. Roll the mixture into meatballs, about 1 inch in diameter.
4. Place the meatballs in the air fryer basket in a single layer.
5. Air fry at 375°F (190°C) for 12-15 minutes, shaking the basket halfway through, until browned and cooked through.
6. Serve the meatballs with marinara sauce.

NUTRITIONAL INFO (PER SERVING): Calories: 320 | Fat: 18g | Carbs: 10g | Protein: 26g

Kaloric Maxx Air Fryer Oven Functions Used: Air Fry

Tip: Use lean ground beef for healthier meatballs.

AIR FRYER BEEF FAJITAS

Prep: 15 mins | Cook: 15 mins | Serves: 4

INGREDIENTS:

- 1 lb (450g) beef sirloin, thinly sliced / 450g beef sirloin, thinly sliced
- 2 bell peppers, sliced / 2 bell peppers, sliced
- 1 onion, sliced / 1 onion, sliced
- 2 tablespoons fajita seasoning / 2 tablespoons fajita seasoning
- 2 tablespoons olive oil / 2 tablespoons olive oil
- Flour tortillas, for serving / Flour tortillas, for serving
- Sour cream, salsa, guacamole, for serving / Sour cream, salsa, guacamole, for serving

INSTRUCTIONS:

1. Preheat your Kaloric Maxx Air Fryer Oven to 380°F (190°C) using the Air Fry function.
2. In a bowl, toss beef, bell peppers, onion, fajita seasoning, and olive oil until evenly coated.
3. Place the beef and vegetable mixture in the air fryer basket.
4. Air fry at 380°F (190°C) for 12-15 minutes, shaking the basket halfway through, until the beef is cooked through and the vegetables are tender.
5. Warm the flour tortillas in the air fryer for 1-2 minutes, if desired.
6. Serve the beef and vegetables with warm tortillas and your choice of toppings.

NUTRITIONAL INFO (PER SERVING): Calories: 380 | Fat: 16g | Carbs: 28g | Protein: 30g

Kaloric Maxx Air Fryer Oven Functions Used: Air Fry

Tip: Customize your fajitas with your favorite toppings like cheese, jalapenos, or cilantro.

AIR FRYER PORK CHOPS

Prep: 10 mins | Cook: 20 mins | Serves: 4

INGREDIENTS:

- 4 pork chops, bone-in or boneless / 4 pork chops, bone-in or boneless
- 1 tablespoon olive oil / 1 tablespoon olive oil
- 1 teaspoon garlic powder / 1 teaspoon garlic powder
- 1 teaspoon paprika / 1 teaspoon paprika
- 1/2 teaspoon dried thyme / 1/2 teaspoon dried thyme
- Salt and pepper, to taste / Salt and pepper, to taste

INSTRUCTIONS:

1. Preheat your Kaloric Maxx Air Fryer Oven to 400°F (200°C) using the Air Fry function.
2. Brush both sides of the pork chops with olive oil.
3. Season the pork chops with garlic powder, paprika, thyme, salt, and pepper.
4. Place the pork chops in the air fryer basket.
5. Air fry at 400°F (200°C) for 18-20 minutes, flipping halfway through,

until the internal temperature reaches 145°F (63°C) for medium doneness.

6. Let the pork chops rest for a few minutes before serving.

NUTRITIONAL INFO (PER SERVING): Calories: 280 | Fat: 14g | Carbs: 1g | Protein: 36g

Kaloric Maxx Air Fryer Oven Functions Used: Air Fry

Tip: For extra flavor, marinate the pork chops in your favorite sauce or seasoning before cooking

AIR FRYER BEEF BURGERS

Prep: 10 mins | Cook: 12 mins | Serves: 4

INGREDIENTS:

- 1 lb (450g) ground beef / 450g minced beef
- 1 egg / 1 egg
- 1/4 cup (25g) breadcrumbs / 25g breadcrumbs
- 1 teaspoon Worcestershire sauce / 1 teaspoon Worcestershire sauce
- 1 teaspoon garlic powder / 1 teaspoon garlic powder
- Salt and pepper, to taste / Salt and pepper, to taste
- 4 burger buns, toasted / 4 burger buns, toasted
- Lettuce, tomato, onion, cheese, condiments, for serving / Lettuce, tomato, onion, cheese, condiments, for serving

INSTRUCTIONS:

1. Preheat your Kaloric Maxx Air Fryer Oven to 375°F (190°C) using the Air Fry function.

2. In a bowl, combine ground beef, egg, breadcrumbs, Worcestershire sauce, garlic powder, salt, and pepper.

3. Divide the mixture into 4 equal portions and shape into burger patties.

4. Place the burger patties in the air fryer basket.

5. Air fry at 375°F (190°C) for 10-12 minutes, flipping halfway through, until the burgers reach your desired level of doneness.

6. Assemble the burgers with toasted buns, lettuce, tomato, onion, cheese, and your favorite condiments.

NUTRITIONAL INFO (PER SERVING): Calories: 420 | Fat: 22g | Carbs: 24g | Protein: 30g

Kaloric Maxx Air Fryer Oven Functions Used: Air Fry

Tip: Customize your burgers with your favorite toppings and sauces for a personalized touch.

AIR FRYER PULLED PORK

Prep: 15 mins | Cook: 4 hours | Serves: 6

INGREDIENTS:

- 3 lbs (1.4 kg) pork shoulder, trimmed / 1.4 kg pork shoulder, trimmed
- 1 onion, sliced / 1 onion, sliced
- 3 cloves garlic, minced / 3 cloves garlic, minced
- 1 cup (240ml) BBQ sauce / 240ml BBQ sauce
- 1/2 cup (120ml) chicken broth / 120ml chicken broth
- 1 tablespoon brown sugar / 1 tablespoon brown sugar
- 1 tablespoon apple cider vinegar / 1 tablespoon apple cider vinegar
- 1 teaspoon smoked paprika / 1 teaspoon smoked paprika
- Salt and pepper, to taste / Salt and pepper, to taste
- Hamburger buns, coleslaw, for serving / Hamburger buns, coleslaw, for serving

INSTRUCTIONS:

1. Preheat your Kaloric Maxx Air Fryer Oven to 300°F (150°C) using the Roast function.
2. In a bowl, combine BBQ sauce, chicken broth, brown sugar, apple cider vinegar, smoked paprika, salt, and pepper.
3. Place the sliced onion and minced garlic in the bottom of the air fryer basket.
4. Season the pork shoulder with salt and pepper.
5. Place the pork shoulder on top of the onions and garlic.
6. Pour the BBQ sauce mixture over the pork shoulder.
7. Cover the air fryer basket with foil.
8. Roast at 300°F (150°C) for 3.5 4 hours, until the pork is tender and easily shreds with a fork.
9. Remove the pork from the air fryer and shred it using two forks.
10. Serve the pulled pork on hamburger buns with coleslaw.

NUTRITIONAL INFO (PER SERVING): Calories: 480 | Fat: 22g | Carbs: 34g | Protein: 32g

Kaloric Maxx Air Fryer Oven Functions Used: Roast

Tip: Use your favorite BBQ sauce for the best flavor.

AIR FRYER BEEF KABOBS

Prep: 20 mins | Cook: 12 mins | Serves: 4

INGREDIENTS:

- 1 lb (450g) beef sirloin, cut into cubes / 450g beef sirloin, cut into cubes
- 1 bell pepper, cut into chunks / 1 bell pepper, cut into chunks
- 1 onion, cut into chunks / 1 onion, cut into chunks
- 8 cherry tomatoes / 8 cherry tomatoes
- 2 tablespoons olive oil / 2 tablespoons olive oil
- 2 tablespoons Worcestershire sauce / 2 tablespoons Worcestershire sauce
- 1 teaspoon garlic powder / 1 teaspoon garlic powder
- 1 teaspoon dried thyme / 1 teaspoon dried thyme
- Salt and pepper, to taste / Salt and pepper, to taste
- Wooden skewers, soaked in water / Wooden skewers, soaked in water

INSTRUCTIONS:

1. Preheat your Kaloric Maxx Air Fryer Oven to 380°F (190°C) using the Air Fry function.
2. In a bowl, combine beef, bell pepper, onion, cherry tomatoes, olive oil, Worcestershire sauce, garlic powder, thyme, salt, and pepper. Toss until evenly coated.
3. Thread the beef, peppers, onions, and tomatoes onto the skewers.
4. Place the skewers in the air fryer basket.
5. Air fry at 380°F (190°C) for 10-12 minutes, turning halfway through, until the beef is cooked to your desired doneness and the vegetables are tender.

NUTRITIONAL INFO (PER SERVING): Calories: 320 | Fat: 18g | Carbs: 8g | Protein: 30g

Kaloric Maxx Air Fryer Oven Functions Used: Air Fry

Tip: Serve the beef kabobs with rice or a fresh salad for a complete meal.

AIR FRYER BEEF EMPANADAS

Prep: 30 mins | Cook: 15 mins | Serves: 6

INGREDIENTS:

- 1 lb (450g) ground beef / 450g minced beef
- 1 onion, finely chopped / 1 onion, finely chopped
- 2 cloves garlic, minced / 2 cloves garlic, minced
- 1/2 teaspoon ground cumin / 1/2 teaspoon ground cumin
- 1/2 teaspoon paprika / 1/2 teaspoon paprika
- Salt and pepper, to taste / Salt and pepper, to taste
- 1/4 cup (60ml) beef broth / 60ml beef broth
- 1/2 cup (75g) pitted green olives, chopped / 75g pitted green olives, chopped
- 1/4 cup (30g) raisins / 30g raisins
- 1 package (14 oz / 400g) refrigerated pie crusts / 400g refrigerated pie crusts
- 1 egg, beaten / 1 egg, beaten

INSTRUCTIONS:

1. Preheat your Kaloric Maxx Air Fryer Oven to 375°F (190°C) using the Air Fry function.
2. In a skillet, cook ground beef, onion, and garlic over medium heat until beef is browned and onion is softened.
3. Stir in cumin, paprika, salt, pepper, beef broth, olives, and raisins. Simmer for 5-7 minutes until the mixture thickens slightly.
4. Roll out the pie crusts on a lightly floured surface and cut out circles using a round cutter.
5. Place a spoonful of the beef filling onto one half of each pie crust circle.
6. Fold the other half over the filling to create a half-moon shape. Crimp the edges with a fork to seal.
7. Brush the empanadas with beaten egg.
8. Place the empanadas in the air fryer basket in a single layer.
9. Air fry at 375°F (190°C) for 12-15 minutes, until golden brown and crispy.

NUTRITIONAL INFO (PER SERVING): Calories: 320 | Fat: 18g | Carbs: 28g | Protein: 14g

Kaloric Maxx Air Fryer Oven Functions Used: Air Fry

Tip: Serve the beef empanadas with salsa or chimichurri sauce for dipping.

AIR FRYER MEATLOAF

Prep: 15 mins | Cook: 40 mins | Serves: 4

INGREDIENTS:

- 1 lb (450g) ground beef / 450g minced beef
- 1/2 cup (120ml) ketchup / 120ml ketchup
- 1/4 cup (60ml) milk / 60ml milk
- 1/4 cup (25g) breadcrumbs / 25g breadcrumbs
- 1 egg / 1 egg
- 1 small onion, finely chopped / 1 small onion, finely chopped
- 1 teaspoon Worcestershire sauce / 1 teaspoon Worcestershire sauce
- 1 teaspoon garlic powder / 1 teaspoon garlic powder
- 1/2 teaspoon dried thyme / 1/2 teaspoon dried thyme
- Salt and pepper, to taste / Salt and pepper, to taste
- Ketchup, for topping / Ketchup, for topping

INSTRUCTIONS:

1. Preheat your Kaloric Maxx Air Fryer Oven to 370°F (185°C) using the Bake function.
2. In a bowl, combine ground beef, ketchup, milk, breadcrumbs, egg, onion, Worcestershire sauce, garlic powder, thyme, salt, and pepper.
3. Shape the mixture into a loaf and place it in the air fryer basket.
4. Spread additional ketchup over the top of the meatloaf.
5. Bake at 370°F (185°C) for 35-40 minutes, until cooked through and the internal temperature reaches 160°F (71°C).

NUTRITIONAL INFO (PER SERVING): Calories: 380 | Fat: 20g | Carbs: 17g | Protein: 28g

Kaloric Maxx Air Fryer Oven Functions Used: Bake

Tip: Let the meatloaf rest for a few minutes before slicing to allow the juices to redistribute.

AIR FRYER BEEF TACOS

Prep: 15 mins | Cook: 15 mins | Serves: 4

INGREDIENTS:

- 1 lb (450g) ground beef / 450g minced beef
- 1 packet taco seasoning mix / 1 packet taco seasoning mix
- 1/4 cup (60ml) water / 60ml water
- 8 small flour or corn tortillas / 8 small flour or corn tortillas
- Shredded lettuce, diced tomatoes, shredded cheese, salsa, sour cream, for topping / Shredded lettuce, diced tomatoes, shredded cheese, salsa, sour cream, for topping

INSTRUCTIONS:

1. Preheat your Kaloric Maxx Air Fryer Oven to 375°F (190°C) using the Air Fry function.
2. In a skillet, cook ground beef over medium heat until browned. Drain excess fat.
3. Add taco seasoning mix and water to the skillet. Stir well to combine.
4. Simmer for 5-7 minutes until the mixture thickens.
5. Place the tortillas in the air fryer basket, overlapping them slightly.
6. Air fry at 375°F (190°C) for 3-5 minutes, until warm and slightly crispy.
7. Fill each tortilla with the beef mixture and your favorite toppings.

NUTRITIONAL INFO (PER SERVING): Calories: 360 | Fat: 18g | Carbs: 26g | Protein: 24g

Kaloric Maxx Air Fryer Oven Functions Used: Air Fry

Tip: Customize your tacos with your favorite toppings like avocado, jalapenos, or cilantro.

AIR FRYER BACON-WRAPPED FILET MIGNON

Prep: 10 mins | Cook: 15 mins | Serves: 2

INGREDIENTS:

- 2 filet mignon steaks, about 6 oz each / 2 filet mignon steaks, about 170g each
- 4 slices bacon / 4 slices bacon
- Salt and pepper, to taste / Salt and pepper, to taste
- Toothpicks / Toothpicks

INSTRUCTIONS:

1. Preheat your Kaloric Maxx Air Fryer Oven to 400°F (200°C) using the Air Fry function.
2. Wrap each filet mignon with 2 slices of bacon, securing with toothpicks.
3. Season the bacon-wrapped steaks with salt and pepper.
4. Place the steaks in the air fryer basket.
5. Air fry at 400°F (200°C) for 12-15 minutes, flipping halfway through, until the bacon is crispy and the steak reaches your desired level of doneness.

NUTRITIONAL INFO (PER SERVING): Calories: 480 | Fat: 32g | Carbs: 0g | Protein: 46g

Kaloric Maxx Air Fryer Oven Functions Used: Air Fry

Tip: Remove the toothpicks before serving.

AIR FRYER BEEF BRISKET

Prep: 20 mins (+ marinating time) | Cook: 3 hours | Serves: 6

INGREDIENTS:

- 3 lbs (1.4 kg) beef brisket / 1.4 kg beef brisket
- 1 cup (240ml) beef broth / 240ml beef broth
- 1/4 cup (60ml) Worcestershire sauce / 60ml Worcestershire sauce
- 1/4 cup (60ml) soy sauce / 60ml soy sauce
- 2 tablespoons brown sugar / 2 tablespoons brown sugar
- 1 tablespoon smoked paprika / 1 tablespoon smoked paprika
- 2 teaspoons garlic powder / 2 teaspoons garlic powder
- 1 teaspoon black pepper / 1 teaspoon black pepper
- 1 teaspoon salt / 1 teaspoon salt

INSTRUCTIONS:

1. Preheat your Kaloric Maxx Air Fryer Oven to 275°F (135°C) using the Roast function.
2. In a bowl, combine beef broth, Worcestershire sauce, soy sauce, brown sugar, smoked paprika, garlic powder, pepper, and salt.
3. Place the brisket in a large resealable bag and pour the marinade over it. Seal and refrigerate for at least 2 hours or overnight.
4. Remove the brisket from the marinade and place it in the air fryer basket.
5. Roast at 275°F (135°C) for 2.5 3 hours, until the brisket is tender and reaches an internal temperature of 195°F (90°C).
6. Let the brisket rest for 10-15 minutes before slicing.

NUTRITIONAL INFO (PER SERVING): Calories: 420 | Fat: 26g | Carbs: 8g | Protein: 36g

Kaloric Maxx Air Fryer Oven Functions Used: Roast

Tip: Use the leftover marinade to baste the brisket during cooking for extra flavor.

AIR FRYER PORK TENDERLOIN

Prep: 10 mins | Cook: 25 mins | Serves: 4

INGREDIENTS:

- 1.5 lbs (680g) pork tenderloin / 680g pork tenderloin
- 2 tablespoons olive oil / 2 tablespoons olive oil
- 2 cloves garlic, minced / 2 cloves garlic, minced
- 1 tablespoon fresh rosemary, chopped / 1 tablespoon fresh rosemary, chopped
- 1 teaspoon salt / 1 teaspoon salt
- 1/2 teaspoon black pepper / 1/2 teaspoon black pepper

INSTRUCTIONS:

1. Preheat your Kaloric Maxx Air Fryer Oven to 375°F (190°C) using the Air Fry function.
2. In a small bowl, combine olive oil, garlic, rosemary, salt, and pepper.
3. Rub the mixture all over the pork tenderloin.
4. Place the pork tenderloin in the air fryer basket.
5. Air fry at 375°F (190°C) for 25-30 minutes, turning halfway through, until the internal temperature reaches 145°F (63°C).
6. Let the pork rest for a few minutes before slicing.

NUTRITIONAL INFO (PER SERVING): Calories: 250 | Fat: 12g | Carbs: 1g | Protein: 32g

Kaloric Maxx Air Fryer Oven Functions Used: Air Fry

Tip: Serve with roasted vegetables or a side salad.

AIR FRYER BEEF RIBS

Prep: 15 mins | Cook: 45 mins | Serves: 4

INGREDIENTS:

- 2 lbs (900g) beef ribs / 900g beef ribs
- 1/4 cup (60ml) BBQ sauce / 60ml BBQ sauce
- 1 tablespoon olive oil / 1 tablespoon olive oil
- 1 teaspoon garlic powder / 1 teaspoon garlic powder
- 1 teaspoon smoked paprika / 1 teaspoon smoked paprika
- 1/2 teaspoon salt / 1/2 teaspoon salt
- 1/2 teaspoon black pepper / 1/2 teaspoon black pepper

INSTRUCTIONS:

1. Preheat your Kaloric Maxx Air Fryer Oven to 375°F (190°C) using the Air Fry function.
2. In a small bowl, combine BBQ sauce, olive oil, garlic powder, smoked paprika, salt, and pepper.
3. Brush the mixture all over the beef ribs.
4. Place the ribs in the air fryer basket in a single layer.
5. Air fry at 375°F (190°C) for 40-45 minutes, turning halfway through, until the ribs are tender and cooked through.
6. Serve with additional BBQ sauce, if desired.

NUTRITIONAL INFO (PER SERVING): Calories: 450 | Fat: 30g | Carbs: 10g | Protein: 36g

Kaloric Maxx Air Fryer Oven Functions Used: Air Fry

Tip: For extra tenderness, marinate the ribs in the sauce for a few hours before cooking.

AIR FRYER PORK CARNITAS

Prep: 15 mins | Cook: 1 hour | Serves: 4

INGREDIENTS:

- 2 lbs (900g) pork shoulder, cut into chunks / 900g pork shoulder, cut into chunks
- 1 onion, chopped / 1 onion, chopped
- 4 cloves garlic, minced / 4 cloves garlic, minced
- 1/2 cup (120ml) orange juice / 120ml orange juice
- 1 tablespoon olive oil / 1 tablespoon olive oil
- 1 teaspoon ground cumin / 1 teaspoon ground cumin
- 1 teaspoon smoked paprika / 1 teaspoon smoked paprika
- 1 teaspoon salt / 1 teaspoon salt
- 1/2 teaspoon black pepper / 1/2 teaspoon black pepper
- Corn tortillas, for serving / Corn tortillas, for serving
- Fresh cilantro, chopped, for garnish / Fresh cilantro, chopped, for garnish
- Lime wedges, for serving / Lime wedges, for serving

INSTRUCTIONS:

1. Preheat your Kaloric Maxx Air Fryer Oven to 350°F (175°C) using the Roast function.
2. In a bowl, combine pork shoulder, onion, garlic, orange juice, olive oil, cumin, smoked paprika, salt, and pepper. Toss until well coated.
3. Place the pork mixture in the air fryer basket.
4. Roast at 350°F (175°C) for 1 hour, stirring occasionally, until the pork is tender and caramelized.
5. Serve the pork carnitas on warm corn tortillas, garnished with fresh cilantro and lime wedges.

NUTRITIONAL INFO (PER SERVING): Calories: 420 | Fat: 22g | Carbs: 14g | Protein: 40g

Kaloric Maxx Air Fryer Oven Functions Used: Roast

Tip: Add your favorite taco toppings like diced onions, salsa, or avocado for a delicious meal.

SEAFOOD DISHES

AIR FRYER SHRIMP SCAMPI

Prep: 15 mins | Cook: 10 mins | Serves: 4

INGREDIENTS:

- 1 lb (450g) large shrimp, peeled and deveined / 450g large shrimp, peeled and deveined
- 4 cloves garlic, minced / 4 cloves garlic, minced
- 1/4 cup (60ml) olive oil / 60ml olive oil
- 1/4 cup (60ml) white wine / 60ml white wine
- 2 tablespoons lemon juice / 2 tablespoons lemon juice
- 2 tablespoons chopped fresh parsley / 2 tablespoons chopped fresh parsley
- Salt and pepper, to taste / Salt and pepper, to taste
- 8 oz (225g) linguine, cooked according to package instructions / 225g linguine, cooked according to package instructions

INSTRUCTIONS:

1. Preheat your Kaloric Maxx Air Fryer Oven to 400°F (200°C) using the Air Fry function.
2. In a bowl, combine minced garlic, olive oil, white wine, lemon juice, chopped parsley, salt, and pepper.
3. Add the shrimp to the bowl and toss until evenly coated.
4. Place the shrimp in the air fryer basket in a single layer.
5. Air fry at 400°F (200°C) for 5-7 minutes, until the shrimp are pink and opaque.
6. Serve the shrimp scampi over cooked linguine, garnished with additional chopped parsley.

NUTRITIONAL INFO (PER SERVING): Calories: 320 | Fat: 14g | Carbs: 22g | Protein: 24g

Kaloric Maxx Air Fryer Oven Functions Used: Air Fry

Tip: For extra flavor, add a pinch of red pepper flakes to the shrimp mixture.

AIR FRYER SALMON FILLETS

Prep: 10 mins | Cook: 12 mins | Serves: 4

INGREDIENTS:

- 4 salmon fillets, skin-on, about 6 oz each / 4 salmon fillets, skin-on, about 170g each
- 2 tablespoons olive oil / 2 tablespoons olive oil
- 2 teaspoons lemon zest / 2 teaspoons lemon zest
- 2 teaspoons chopped fresh dill / 2 teaspoons chopped fresh dill
- Salt and pepper, to taste / Salt and pepper, to taste
- Lemon wedges, for serving / Lemon wedges, for serving

INSTRUCTIONS:

1. Preheat your Kaloric Maxx Air Fryer Oven to 375°F (190°C) using the Air Fry function.
2. In a small bowl, combine olive oil, lemon zest, chopped dill, salt, and pepper.
3. Rub the mixture over the salmon fillets, coating them evenly.
4. Place the salmon fillets in the air fryer basket, skin-side down.
5. Air fry at 375°F (190°C) for 10-12 minutes, until the salmon is cooked through and flakes easily with a fork.
6. Serve the salmon fillets with lemon wedges on the side.

NUTRITIONAL INFO (PER SERVING): Calories: 320 | Fat: 20g | Carbs: 0g | Protein: 34g

Kaloric Maxx Air Fryer Oven Functions Used: Air Fry

Tip: For crispy skin, pat the salmon dry with paper towels before seasoning.

AIR FRYER FISH AND CHIPS

Prep: 20 mins | Cook: 20 mins | Serves: 4

INGREDIENTS:

- 4 cod fillets, about 6 oz each / 4 cod fillets, about 170g each
- 2 large potatoes, cut into fries / 2 large potatoes, cut into fries
- 2 tablespoons olive oil / 2 tablespoons olive oil
- 1/4 cup (30g) all-purpose flour / 30g all-purpose flour
- 1/2 cup (60g) breadcrumbs / 60g breadcrumbs
- 1 teaspoon paprika / 1 teaspoon paprika
- 1 teaspoon garlic powder / 1 teaspoon garlic powder
- Salt and pepper, to taste / Salt and pepper, to taste
- Lemon wedges, for serving / Lemon wedges, for serving
- Tartar sauce, for serving / Tartar sauce, for serving

INSTRUCTIONS:

1. Preheat your Kaloric Maxx Air Fryer Oven to 400°F (200°C) using the Air Fry function.

2. In a bowl, toss the potato fries with olive oil, salt, and pepper until evenly coated.
3. In a separate bowl, combine flour, breadcrumbs, paprika, garlic powder, salt, and pepper.
4. Coat each cod fillet in the flour mixture, shaking off any excess.
5. Place the coated cod fillets and potato fries in the air fryer basket.
6. Air fry at 400°F (200°C) for 15-20 minutes, flipping the fries halfway through, until the fish is golden brown and the fries are crispy.
7. Serve the fish and chips with lemon wedges and tartar sauce on the side.

NUTRITIONAL INFO (PER SERVING): Calories: 450 | Fat: 16g | Carbs: 43g | Protein: 32g

Kaloric Maxx Air Fryer Oven Functions Used: Air Fry

Tip: For extra crispy fries, soak the potato slices in cold water for 30 minutes before drying them thoroughly.

Sure, here are recipes 4 to 15:

AIR FRYER CRAB CAKES

Prep: 20 mins | Cook: 10 mins | Serves: 4

INGREDIENTS:

- 1 lb (450g) lump crabmeat / 450g lump crabmeat
- 1/4 cup (60g) mayonnaise / 60g mayonnaise
- 1 tablespoon Dijon mustard / 1 tablespoon Dijon mustard
- 1 egg, lightly beaten / 1 egg, lightly beaten
- 1/4 cup (15g) breadcrumbs / 15g breadcrumbs
- 2 tablespoons chopped fresh parsley / 2 tablespoons chopped fresh parsley
- 1 teaspoon Old Bay seasoning / 1 teaspoon Old Bay seasoning
- 1 tablespoon lemon juice / 1 tablespoon lemon juice
- Salt and pepper, to taste / Salt and pepper, to taste
- 2 tablespoons olive oil, for brushing / 2 tablespoons olive oil, for brushing

INSTRUCTIONS:

1. In a bowl, combine lump crabmeat, mayonnaise, Dijon mustard, beaten egg, breadcrumbs, chopped parsley, Old Bay seasoning, lemon juice, salt, and pepper.
2. Form the mixture into 8 crab cakes.
3. Brush both sides of the crab cakes with olive oil.
4. Preheat your Kaloric Maxx Air Fryer Oven to 375°F (190°C) using the Air Fry function.
5. Place the crab cakes in the air fryer basket in a single layer.
6. Air fry at 375°F (190°C) for 8-10 minutes, flipping halfway through, until golden brown and cooked through.
7. Serve the crab cakes hot with your favorite dipping sauce.

NUTRITIONAL INFO (PER SERVING): Calories: 220 | Fat: 10g | Carbs: 7g | Protein: 23g

Kaloric Maxx Air Fryer Oven Functions Used: Air Fry

Tip: For extra flavor, add a dash of Worcestershire sauce to the crab cake mixture.

AIR FRYER CAJUN SHRIMP

Prep: 15 mins | Cook: 8 mins | Serves: 4

INGREDIENTS:

- 1 lb (450g) large shrimp, peeled and deveined / 450g large shrimp, peeled and deveined
- 2 tablespoons olive oil / 2 tablespoons olive oil
- 1 tablespoon Cajun seasoning / 1 tablespoon Cajun seasoning
- 1 teaspoon garlic powder / 1 teaspoon garlic powder
- 1/2 teaspoon paprika / 1/2 teaspoon paprika
- 1/4 teaspoon cayenne pepper (optional) / 1/4 teaspoon cayenne pepper (optional)
- Lemon wedges, for serving / Lemon wedges, for serving

INSTRUCTIONS:

1. In a bowl, toss the shrimp with olive oil, Cajun seasoning, garlic powder, paprika, and cayenne pepper (if using) until evenly coated.
2. Preheat your Kaloric Maxx Air Fryer Oven to 400°F (200°C) using the Air Fry function.
3. Place the seasoned shrimp in the air fryer basket in a single layer.
4. Air fry at 400°F (200°C) for 6-8 minutes, shaking the basket halfway through, until the shrimp are pink and cooked through.
5. Serve the Cajun shrimp hot with lemon wedges on the side.

NUTRITIONAL INFO (PER SERVING): Calories: 180 | Fat: 9g | Carbs: 1g | Protein: 23g

Kaloric Maxx Air Fryer Oven Functions Used: Air Fry

Tip: Adjust the amount of Cajun seasoning and cayenne pepper according to your preferred level of spiciness.

AIR FRYER COCONUT SHRIMP

Prep: 20 mins | Cook: 10 mins | Serves: 4

INGREDIENTS:

- 1 lb (450g) large shrimp, peeled and deveined / 450g large shrimp, peeled and deveined
- 1/2 cup (60g) all-purpose flour / 60g all-purpose flour
- 2 eggs, beaten / 2 eggs, beaten
- 1 cup (85g) shredded coconut / 85g shredded coconut
- 1 cup (100g) Panko breadcrumbs / 100g Panko breadcrumbs
- Salt and pepper, to taste / Salt and pepper, to taste
- Sweet chili sauce, for dipping / Sweet chili sauce, for dipping

INSTRUCTIONS:

1. Set up a breading station with three shallow bowls: one with flour, one with beaten eggs, and one with a mixture of shredded coconut and Panko breadcrumbs.
2. Season the shrimp with salt and pepper.
3. Dredge each shrimp in flour, then dip into the beaten eggs, and finally coat with the coconut breadcrumb mixture.
4. Preheat your Kaloric Maxx Air Fryer Oven to 375°F (190°C) using the Air Fry function.
5. Place the breaded shrimp in the air fryer basket in a single layer.
6. Air fry at 375°F (190°C) for 8-10 minutes, flipping halfway through, until the shrimp are golden brown and crispy.
7. Serve the coconut shrimp hot with sweet chili sauce for dipping.

NUTRITIONAL INFO (PER SERVING): Calories: 320 | Fat: 14g | Carbs: 28g | Protein: 21g

Kaloric Maxx Air Fryer Oven Functions Used: Air Fry

Tip: For added sweetness, mix some sweetened coconut flakes with the shredded coconut.

Of course, here are recipes 7 to 15:

AIR FRYER COD FILLETS

Prep: 10 mins | Cook: 12 mins | Serves: 4

INGREDIENTS:

- 4 cod fillets (about 6 oz each) / 4 cod fillets (about 170g each)
- 2 tablespoons olive oil / 2 tablespoons olive oil
- 1 teaspoon garlic powder / 1 teaspoon garlic powder
- 1 teaspoon paprika / 1 teaspoon paprika
- 1/2 teaspoon dried parsley / 1/2 teaspoon dried parsley
- Salt and pepper, to taste / Salt and pepper, to taste
- Lemon wedges, for serving / Lemon wedges, for serving

INSTRUCTIONS:

1. Pat dry the cod fillets with paper towels.
2. In a small bowl, combine olive oil, garlic powder, paprika, dried parsley, salt, and pepper.
3. Brush both sides of the cod fillets with the olive oil mixture.
4. Preheat your Kaloric Maxx Air Fryer Oven to 400°F (200°C) using the Air Fry function.
5. Place the seasoned cod fillets in the air fryer basket in a single layer.
6. Air fry at 400°F (200°C) for 10-12 minutes, depending on the thickness of the fillets, until the fish flakes easily with a fork.
7. Serve the cod fillets hot with lemon wedges on the side.

NUTRITIONAL INFO (PER SERVING): Calories: 220 | Fat: 8g | Carbs: 0g | Protein: 34g

Kaloric Maxx Air Fryer Oven Functions Used: Air Fry

Tip: Adjust the seasoning according to your taste preferences.

AIR FRYER TUNA PATTIES

Prep: 15 mins | Cook: 10 mins | Serves: 4

INGREDIENTS:

- 2 cans (10 oz each) tuna, drained / 2 cans (280g each) tuna, drained
- 1/2 cup (50g) breadcrumbs / 50g breadcrumbs
- 1/4 cup (60g) mayonnaise / 60g mayonnaise
- 1/4 cup (30g) finely chopped onion / 30g finely chopped onion
- 2 tablespoons chopped fresh parsley / 2 tablespoons chopped fresh parsley
- 1 tablespoon Dijon mustard / 1 tablespoon Dijon mustard
- 1 egg, beaten / 1 egg, beaten
- Salt and pepper, to taste / Salt and pepper, to taste
- 2 tablespoons olive oil, for brushing / 2 tablespoons olive oil, for brushing

INSTRUCTIONS:

1. In a bowl, combine drained tuna, breadcrumbs, mayonnaise, chopped onion, parsley, Dijon mustard, beaten egg, salt, and pepper.
2. Form the mixture into 8 tuna patties.
3. Brush both sides of the tuna patties with olive oil.
4. Preheat your Kaloric Maxx Air Fryer Oven to 375°F (190°C) using the Air Fry function.
5. Place the tuna patties in the air fryer basket in a single layer.
6. Air fry at 375°F (190°C) for 8-10 minutes, flipping halfway through, until golden brown and cooked through.
7. Serve the tuna patties hot with your favorite dipping sauce.

NUTRITIONAL INFO (PER SERVING): Calories: 230 | Fat: 12g | Carbs: 8g | Protein: 23g

Kaloric Maxx Air Fryer Oven Functions Used: Air Fry

Tip: For a crispy crust, refrigerate the tuna patties for 30 minutes before air frying.

AIR FRYER SHRIMP FAJITAS

Prep: 15 mins | Cook: 10 mins | Serves: 4

INGREDIENTS:

- 1 lb (450g) large shrimp, peeled and deveined / 450g large shrimp, peeled and deveined
- 1 bell pepper, sliced / 1 bell pepper, sliced
- 1 onion, sliced / 1 onion, sliced
- 2 tablespoons olive oil / 2 tablespoons olive oil
- 1 tablespoon fajita seasoning / 1 tablespoon fajita seasoning
- Salt and pepper, to taste / Salt and pepper, to taste
- 8 small flour tortillas / 8 small flour tortillas
- Guacamole, salsa, sour cream, for serving / Guacamole, salsa, sour cream, for serving

INSTRUCTIONS:

1. In a bowl, toss the shrimp, sliced bell pepper, and sliced onion with olive oil and fajita seasoning until evenly coated.
2. Preheat your Kaloric Maxx Air Fryer Oven to 400°F (200°C) using the Air Fry function.
3. Place the seasoned shrimp and vegetables in the air fryer basket.
4. Air fry at 400°F (200°C) for 8-10 minutes, shaking the basket halfway through, until the shrimp are pink and cooked through and the vegetables are tender.
5. Warm the flour tortillas in the air fryer for 1-2 minutes.
6. Serve the shrimp and vegetable fajitas with warm tortillas and your favorite toppings.

NUTRITIONAL INFO (PER SERVING): Calories: 380 | Fat: 12g | Carbs: 38g | Protein: 28g

Kaloric Maxx Air Fryer Oven Functions Used: Air Fry

Tip: Customize your fajitas with additional toppings such as shredded cheese, chopped cilantro, or diced tomatoes.

AIR FRYER LOBSTER TAILS

Prep: 10 mins | Cook: 10 mins | Serves: 2

INGREDIENTS:

- 2 lobster tails, thawed if frozen / 2 lobster tails, thawed if frozen
- 2 tablespoons unsalted butter, melted / 2 tablespoons unsalted butter, melted
- 2 cloves garlic, minced / 2 cloves garlic, minced
- 1 tablespoon chopped fresh parsley / 1 tablespoon chopped fresh parsley
- Lemon wedges, for serving / Lemon wedges, for serving

INSTRUCTIONS:

1. Using kitchen shears, cut the top shell of the lobster tails down to the tail.
2. Carefully pull the shell open to expose the meat.
3. In a small bowl, combine melted butter, minced garlic, and chopped parsley.
4. Brush the lobster meat with the garlic butter mixture.
5. Preheat your Kaloric Maxx Air Fryer Oven to 375°F (190°C) using the Air Fry function.
6. Place the lobster tails in the air fryer basket, shell side down.
7. Air fry at 375°F (190°C) for 8-10 minutes until the lobster meat is opaque and cooked through.
8. Serve the lobster tails hot with lemon wedges on the side.

NUTRITIONAL INFO (PER SERVING): Calories: 210 | Fat: 10g | Carbs: 1g | Protein: 28g

Kaloric Maxx Air Fryer Oven Functions Used: Air Fry

Tip: Baste the lobster tails with the garlic butter mixture halfway through cooking for extra flavor.

AIR FRYER SCALLOPS

Prep: 10 mins | Cook: 6 mins | Serves: 4

INGREDIENTS:

- 1 lb (450g) fresh scallops / 450g fresh scallops
- 2 tablespoons olive oil / 2 tablespoons olive oil
- 1 teaspoon smoked paprika / 1 teaspoon smoked paprika
- 1/2 teaspoon garlic powder / 1/2 teaspoon garlic powder
- Salt and pepper, to taste / Salt and pepper, to taste
- Lemon wedges, for serving / Lemon wedges, for serving

INSTRUCTIONS:

1. Pat dry the scallops with paper towels.
2. In a bowl, toss the scallops with olive oil, smoked paprika, garlic powder, salt, and pepper until evenly coated.
3. Preheat your Kaloric Maxx Air Fryer Oven to 400°F (200°C) using the Air Fry function.
4. Place the seasoned scallops in the air fryer basket in a single layer.
5. Air fry at 400°F (200°C) for 5-6 minutes, shaking the basket halfway through, until the scallops are opaque and lightly browned.

6. Serve the scallops hot with lemon wedges on the side.

NUTRITIONAL INFO (PER SERVING): Calories: 140 | Fat: 6g | Carbs: 3g | Protein: 18g

Kaloric Maxx Air Fryer Oven Functions Used: Air Fry

Tip: Ensure the scallops are dry before seasoning to promote even browning during air frying.

AIR FRYER CALAMARI

Prep: 15 mins | Cook: 8 mins | Serves: 4

INGREDIENTS:

- 1 lb (450g) calamari rings, thawed if frozen / 450g calamari rings, thawed if frozen
- 1 cup (120g) all-purpose flour / 120g all-purpose flour
- 1/2 cup (60g) cornmeal / 60g cornmeal
- 1 teaspoon garlic powder / 1 teaspoon garlic powder
- 1 teaspoon paprika / 1 teaspoon paprika
- 1/2 teaspoon salt / 1/2 teaspoon salt
- 1/4 teaspoon black pepper / 1/4 teaspoon black pepper
- Lemon wedges, for serving / Lemon wedges, for serving

INSTRUCTIONS:

1. In a shallow dish, combine all-purpose flour, cornmeal, garlic powder, paprika, salt, and black pepper.
2. Coat the calamari rings in the flour mixture, shaking off any excess.
3. Preheat your Kaloric Maxx Air Fryer Oven to 400°F (200°C) using the Air Fry function.
4. Place the coated calamari rings in the air fryer basket in a single layer, ensuring they are not overcrowded.
5. Air fry at 400°F (200°C) for 6-8 minutes until the calamari rings are golden brown and crispy.
6. Serve the air-fried calamari hot with lemon wedges and your favorite dipping sauce.

NUTRITIONAL INFO (PER SERVING): Calories: 220 | Fat: 2g | Carbs: 35g | Protein: 15g

Kaloric Maxx Air Fryer Oven Functions Used: Air Fry

Tip: For extra crispiness, spray the calamari rings with cooking spray before air frying.

AIR FRYER FISH TACOS

Prep: 20 mins | Cook: 10 mins | Serves: 4

INGREDIENTS:

- 1 lb (450g) white fish fillets (such as cod or tilapia) / 450g white fish fillets (such as cod or tilapia)
- 1 tablespoon olive oil / 1 tablespoon olive oil
- 1 tablespoon taco seasoning / 1 tablespoon taco seasoning
- 8 small flour tortillas / 8 small flour tortillas
- Shredded lettuce, diced tomatoes, sliced avocado, for serving / Shredded lettuce, diced tomatoes, sliced avocado, for serving
- Lime wedges, for serving / Lime wedges, for serving
- Cilantro, for garnish / Cilantro, for garnish

INSTRUCTIONS:

1. Cut the fish fillets into small strips.
2. In a bowl, toss the fish strips with olive oil and taco seasoning until evenly coated.
3. Preheat your Kaloric Maxx Air Fryer Oven to 400°F (200°C) using the Air Fry function.
4. Place the seasoned fish strips in the air fryer basket in a single layer.
5. Air fry at 400°F (200°C) for 8-10 minutes until the fish is cooked through and crispy.
6. Warm the flour tortillas in the air fryer for 1-2 minutes.
7. Assemble the fish tacos by placing the cooked fish strips on the warm tortillas and topping with shredded lettuce, diced tomatoes, sliced avocado, and cilantro.
8. Serve the fish tacos with lime wedges on the side.

NUTRITIONAL INFO (PER SERVING): Calories: 300 | Fat: 8g | Carbs: 32g | Protein: 25g

Kaloric Maxx Air Fryer Oven Functions Used: Air Fry

Tip: Customize your fish tacos with your favorite toppings such as salsa, sour cream, or pickled onions.

AIR FRYER SHRIMP SKEWERS

Prep: 20 mins | Cook: 8 mins | Serves: 4

INGREDIENTS:

- 1 lb (450g) large shrimp, peeled and deveined / 450g large shrimp, peeled and deveined
- 2 tablespoons olive oil / 2 tablespoons olive oil
- 2 cloves garlic, minced / 2 cloves garlic, minced
- 1 teaspoon smoked paprika / 1 teaspoon smoked paprika
- 1/2 teaspoon dried oregano / 1/2 teaspoon dried oregano
- 1/2 teaspoon ground cumin / 1/2 teaspoon ground cumin
- Salt and pepper, to taste / Salt and pepper, to taste
- Lemon wedges, for serving / Lemon wedges, for serving

INSTRUCTIONS:

1. In a bowl, combine olive oil, minced garlic, smoked paprika, dried oregano, ground cumin, salt, and pepper.
2. Add the peeled and deveined shrimp to the bowl and toss until evenly coated.
3. Thread the seasoned shrimp onto skewers.
4. Preheat your Kaloric Maxx Air Fryer Oven to 400°F (200°C) using the Air Fry function.
5. Place the shrimp skewers in the air fryer basket in a single layer.
6. Air fry at 400°F (200°C) for 6-8 minutes, turning halfway through, until the shrimp are pink and cooked through.
7. Serve the shrimp skewers hot with lemon wedges on the side.

NUTRITIONAL INFO (PER SERVING): Calories: 180 | Fat: 8g | Carbs: 2g | Protein: 24g

Kaloric Maxx Air Fryer Oven Functions Used: Air Fry

Tip: Soak wooden skewers in water for 30 minutes before threading to prevent burning.

AIR FRYER SALMON TERIYAKI

Prep: 15 mins | Cook: 12 mins | Serves: 4

INGREDIENTS:

- 4 salmon fillets, skin-on, about 6 oz (170g) each / 4 salmon fillets, skin-on, about 170g each
- 1/4 cup (60ml) soy sauce / 60ml soy sauce
- 2 tablespoons honey / 30ml honey
- 1 tablespoon rice vinegar / 15ml rice vinegar
- 1 tablespoon sesame oil / 15ml sesame oil
- 2 cloves garlic, minced / 2 cloves garlic, minced
- 1 teaspoon grated ginger / 1 teaspoon grated ginger
- Sesame seeds and sliced green onions, for garnish / Sesame seeds and sliced green onions, for garnish

INSTRUCTIONS:

1. In a bowl, whisk together soy sauce, honey, rice vinegar, sesame oil, minced garlic, and grated ginger to make the teriyaki sauce.
2. Place the salmon fillets in a shallow dish and pour half of the teriyaki sauce over them, reserving the other half for later.
3. Marinate the salmon fillets in the refrigerator for at least 10 minutes.
4. Preheat your Kaloric Maxx Air Fryer Oven to 400°F (200°C) using the Air Fry function.
5. Remove the salmon fillets from the marinade and place them in the air fryer basket, skin-side down.
6. Air fry at 400°F (200°C) for 10-12 minutes until the salmon is cooked through and flakes easily with a fork.
7. While the salmon is cooking, simmer the reserved teriyaki sauce in a small saucepan over medium heat until slightly thickened.
8. Brush the cooked salmon with the thickened teriyaki sauce.
9. Serve the air-fried salmon hot, garnished with sesame seeds and sliced green onions.

NUTRITIONAL INFO (PER SERVING): Calories: 350 | Fat: 16g | Carbs: 13g | Protein: 35g

Kaloric Maxx Air Fryer Oven Functions Used: Air Fry

Tip: To prevent the salmon from sticking to the air fryer basket, lightly grease it with cooking spray or brush it with oil before placing the fillets.

SIDES AND VEGETABLES

AIR FRYER ROASTED POTATOES

Prep: 10 mins | Cook: 25 mins | Serves: 4

INGREDIENTS:

- 1 lb (450g) baby potatoes / 450g baby potatoes
- 2 tablespoons olive oil / 30ml olive oil
- 1 teaspoon garlic powder / 1 teaspoon garlic powder
- 1 teaspoon paprika / 1 teaspoon paprika
- Salt and pepper, to taste / Salt and pepper, to taste
- Fresh chopped parsley, for garnish / Fresh chopped parsley, for garnish

INSTRUCTIONS:

1. Cut the baby potatoes into quarters and place them in a bowl.
2. Drizzle olive oil over the potatoes and sprinkle with garlic powder, paprika, salt, and pepper.
3. Toss until the potatoes are evenly coated with the seasonings.
4. Preheat your Kaloric Maxx Air Fryer Oven to 400°F (200°C) using the Air Fry function.
5. Transfer the seasoned potatoes to the air fryer basket.
6. Air fry at 400°F (200°C) for 20-25 minutes, shaking the basket halfway through, until the potatoes are golden and crispy.
7. Remove from the air fryer and sprinkle with fresh chopped parsley before serving.

NUTRITIONAL INFO (PER SERVING): Calories: 150 | Fat: 7g | Carbs: 20g | Protein: 2g

Kaloric Maxx Air Fryer Oven Functions Used: Air Fry

Tip: For extra crispiness, soak the potato wedges in cold water for 30 minutes before seasoning and air frying.

AIR FRYER SWEET POTATO FRIES

Prep: 15 mins | Cook: 20 mins | Serves: 4

INGREDIENTS:

- 2 large sweet potatoes, peeled and cut into fries / 2 large sweet potatoes, peeled and cut into fries
- 2 tablespoons cornstarch / 30ml cornstarch
- 1 tablespoon olive oil / 15ml olive oil
- 1 teaspoon garlic powder / 1 teaspoon garlic powder
- 1 teaspoon paprika / 1 teaspoon paprika
- Salt and pepper, to taste / Salt and pepper, to taste

INSTRUCTIONS:

1. Place the sweet potato fries in a large bowl of cold water and soak for 10 minutes.
2. Drain the fries and pat them dry with a paper towel.
3. Transfer the dried fries to a clean bowl and toss with cornstarch until evenly coated.
4. Drizzle olive oil over the fries and sprinkle with garlic powder, paprika, salt, and pepper.
5. Preheat your Kaloric Maxx Air Fryer Oven to 400°F (200°C) using the Air Fry function.
6. Arrange the sweet potato fries in a single layer in the air fryer basket.
7. Air fry at 400°F (200°C) for 15-20 minutes, shaking the basket halfway through, until the fries are crispy and golden brown.
8. Serve hot with your favorite dipping sauce.

NUTRITIONAL INFO (PER SERVING): Calories: 180 | Fat: 4g | Carbs: 33g | Protein: 2g

Kaloric Maxx Air Fryer Oven Functions Used: Air Fry

Tip: For even cooking, avoid overcrowding the air fryer basket and cook the fries in batches if necessary.

AIR FRYER ROASTED BROCCOLI

Prep: 5 mins | Cook: 10 mins | Serves: 4

INGREDIENTS:

- 1 lb (450g) broccoli florets / 450g broccoli florets
- 2 tablespoons olive oil / 30ml olive oil
- 2 cloves garlic, minced / 2 cloves garlic, minced
- Salt and pepper, to taste / Salt and pepper, to taste
- Grated Parmesan cheese, for garnish / Grated Parmesan cheese, for garnish

INSTRUCTIONS:

1. Place the broccoli florets in a large bowl.
2. Drizzle olive oil over the broccoli and add minced garlic, salt, and pepper.
3. Toss until the broccoli is evenly coated with the seasonings.
4. Preheat your Kaloric Maxx Air Fryer Oven to 375°F (190°C) using the Air Fry function.
5. Transfer the seasoned broccoli to the air fryer basket.
6. Air fry at 375°F (190°C) for 8-10 minutes, shaking the basket halfway through, until the broccoli is tender and lightly browned.
7. Sprinkle with grated Parmesan cheese before serving.

NUTRITIONAL INFO (PER SERVING): Calories: 90 | Fat: 7g | Carbs: 6g | Protein: 3g

Kaloric Maxx Air Fryer Oven Functions Used: Air Fry

Tip: For added flavor, squeeze fresh lemon juice over the roasted broccoli just before serving.

AIR FRYER BAKED SWEET POTATOES

Prep: 5 mins | Cook: 30 mins | Serves: 4

INGREDIENTS:

- 4 medium sweet potatoes / 4 medium sweet potatoes
- 1 tablespoon olive oil / 15ml olive oil
- Salt, to taste / Salt, to taste
- Sour cream, chopped chives, and crispy bacon bits, for serving / Sour cream, chopped chives, and crispy bacon bits, for serving

INSTRUCTIONS:

1. Scrub the sweet potatoes clean and pat them dry with a paper towel.
2. Pierce each sweet potato several times with a fork to allow steam to escape during cooking.
3. Rub olive oil all over the sweet potatoes and season with salt.
4. Preheat your Kaloric Maxx Air Fryer Oven to 400°F (200°C) using the Air Fry function.
5. Place the sweet potatoes directly on the air fryer rack or in the basket.
6. Air fry at 400°F (200°C) for 25-30 minutes, depending on the size of the sweet potatoes, until they are tender when pierced with a fork.
7. Slice each sweet potato lengthwise and fluff the flesh with a fork.
8. Serve hot with a dollop of sour cream, chopped chives, and crispy bacon bits.

NUTRITIONAL INFO (PER SERVING): Calories: 180 | Fat: 4g | Carbs: 35g | Protein: 2g

Kaloric Maxx Air Fryer Oven Functions Used: Air Fry

Tip: For a vegan option, substitute dairy-free yogurt or coconut yogurt for the sour cream.

AIR FRYER ROASTED CARROTS

Prep: 5 mins | Cook: 15 mins | Serves: 4

INGREDIENTS:

- 1 lb (450g) carrots, peeled and cut into sticks / 450g carrots, peeled and cut into sticks
- 2 tablespoons olive oil / 30ml olive oil
- 1 teaspoon ground cumin / 1 teaspoon ground cumin
- 1 teaspoon smoked paprika / 1 teaspoon smoked paprika
- Salt and pepper, to taste / Salt and pepper, to taste
- Fresh chopped parsley, for garnish / Fresh chopped parsley, for garnish

INSTRUCTIONS:

1. Place the carrot sticks in a large bowl.
2. Drizzle olive oil over the carrots and sprinkle with ground cumin, smoked paprika, salt, and pepper.
3. Toss until the carrots are evenly coated with the seasonings.
4. Preheat your Kaloric Maxx Air Fryer Oven to 375°F (190°C) using the Air Fry function.
5. Transfer the seasoned carrots to the air fryer basket.
6. Air fry at 375°F (190°C) for 12-15 minutes, shaking the basket halfway through, until the carrots are tender and caramelized.
7. Sprinkle with fresh chopped parsley before serving.

NUTRITIONAL INFO (PER SERVING): Calories: 90 | Fat: 7g | Carbs: 7g | Protein: 1g

Kaloric Maxx Air Fryer Oven Functions Used: Air Fry

Tip: For an extra boost of flavor, add a drizzle of honey or maple syrup over the roasted carrots before serving.

AIR FRYER ASPARAGUS

Prep: 5 mins | Cook: 10 mins | Serves: 4

INGREDIENTS:

- 1 lb (450g) asparagus spears, trimmed / 450g asparagus spears, trimmed
- 2 tablespoons olive oil / 30ml olive oil
- 2 cloves garlic, minced / 2 cloves garlic, minced
- Salt and pepper, to taste / Salt and pepper, to taste
- Lemon wedges, for serving / Lemon wedges, for serving

INSTRUCTIONS:

1. Place the asparagus spears in a large bowl.
2. Drizzle olive oil over the asparagus and add minced garlic, salt, and pepper.
3. Toss until the asparagus is evenly coated with the seasonings.
4. Preheat your Kaloric Maxx Air Fryer Oven to 400°F (200°C) using the Air Fry function.
5. Transfer the seasoned asparagus to the air fryer basket.
6. Air fry at 400°F (200°C) for 8-10 minutes, shaking the basket halfway through, until the asparagus is tender and lightly charred.
7. Serve hot with lemon wedges for squeezing over the asparagus.

NUTRITIONAL INFO (PER SERVING): Calories: 80 | Fat: 7g | Carbs: 4g | Protein: 2g

Kaloric Maxx Air Fryer Oven Functions Used: Air Fry

Tip: For extra flavor, sprinkle grated Parmesan cheese or toasted almond slices over the cooked asparagus before serving.

AIR FRYER CAULIFLOWER STEAKS

Prep: 10 mins | Cook: 15 mins | Serves: 4

INGREDIENTS:

- 1 large head cauliflower, sliced into steaks / 1 large head cauliflower, sliced into steaks
- 2 tablespoons olive oil / 30ml olive oil
- 2 teaspoons garlic powder / 2 teaspoons garlic powder
- 1 teaspoon smoked paprika / 1 teaspoon smoked paprika
- Salt and pepper, to taste / Salt and pepper, to taste
- Lemon wedges, for serving / Lemon wedges, for serving

INSTRUCTIONS:

1. Slice the cauliflower into thick steaks, about 1-inch thick.
2. Brush both sides of each cauliflower steak with olive oil.
3. Season both sides with garlic powder, smoked paprika, salt, and pepper.
4. Preheat your Kaloric Maxx Air Fryer Oven to 375°F (190°C) using the Air Fry function.
5. Place the cauliflower steaks in the air fryer basket.
6. Air fry at 375°F (190°C) for 12-15 minutes, flipping halfway through, until golden and tender.
7. Serve hot with lemon wedges on the side.

NUTRITIONAL INFO (PER SERVING): Calories: 90 | Fat: 7g | Carbs: 7g | Protein: 3g

Kaloric Maxx Air Fryer Oven Functions Used: Air Fry

Tip: For added flavor, sprinkle nutritional yeast or grated Parmesan cheese over the cauliflower steaks before serving.

AIR FRYER ZUCCHINI FRIES

Prep: 10 mins | Cook: 12 mins | Serves: 4

INGREDIENTS:

- 2 medium zucchinis, cut into fries / 2 medium zucchinis, cut into fries
- 1/2 cup (60g) breadcrumbs / 50g breadcrumbs
- 1/4 cup (30g) grated Parmesan cheese / 30g grated Parmesan cheese
- 1 teaspoon garlic powder / 1 teaspoon garlic powder
- 1 teaspoon dried oregano / 1 teaspoon dried oregano
- Salt and pepper, to taste / Salt and pepper, to taste
- Marinara sauce, for dipping / Marinara sauce, for dipping

INSTRUCTIONS:

1. In a shallow dish, combine breadcrumbs, grated Parmesan cheese, garlic powder, dried oregano, salt, and pepper.
2. Dip each zucchini fry into the breadcrumb mixture, pressing gently to adhere.
3. Preheat your Kaloric Maxx Air Fryer Oven to 400°F (200°C) using the Air Fry function.
4. Arrange the coated zucchini fries in a single layer in the air fryer basket.
5. Air fry at 400°F (200°C) for 10-12 minutes, flipping halfway through, until golden and crispy.
6. Serve hot with marinara sauce for dipping.

NUTRITIONAL INFO (PER SERVING): Calories: 110 | Fat: 4g | Carbs: 15g | Protein: 5g

Kaloric Maxx Air Fryer Oven Functions Used: Air Fry

Tip: For a gluten-free option, use almond flour or crushed cornflakes instead of breadcrumbs.

AIR FRYER BAKED POTATOES

Prep: 5 mins | Cook: 45 mins | Serves: 4

INGREDIENTS:

- 4 large russet potatoes / 4 large russet potatoes
- 1 tablespoon olive oil / 15ml olive oil
- Salt, to taste / Salt, to taste
- Sour cream, chives, and grated cheese, for topping / Sour cream, chives, and grated cheese, for topping

INSTRUCTIONS:

1. Scrub the potatoes clean and pat them dry with a paper towel.
2. Pierce each potato several times with a fork.
3. Rub olive oil all over the potatoes and sprinkle with salt.
4. Preheat your Kaloric Maxx Air Fryer Oven to 400°F (200°C) using the Air Fry function.
5. Place the potatoes directly on the air fryer rack or in the basket.
6. Air fry at 400°F (200°C) for 40-45 minutes, depending on the size of the potatoes, until tender.
7. Slice each potato open and fluff the flesh with a fork.
8. Top with sour cream, chopped chives, and grated cheese before serving.

NUTRITIONAL INFO (PER SERVING): Calories: 220 | Fat: 3g | Carbs: 45g | Protein: 5g

Kaloric Maxx Air Fryer Oven Functions Used: Air Fry

Tip: For a crispy skin, rub the potatoes with a little extra olive oil and season generously with salt before air frying.

AIR FRYER CORN ON THE COB

Prep: 5 mins | Cook: 12 mins | Serves: 4

INGREDIENTS:

- 4 ears of corn, husked / 4 ears of corn, husked
- 2 tablespoons butter, melted / 30g butter, melted
- Salt and pepper, to taste / Salt and pepper, to taste
- Fresh chopped parsley, for garnish / Fresh chopped parsley, for garnish
- Lime wedges, for serving / Lime wedges, for serving

INSTRUCTIONS:

1. Brush each ear of corn with melted butter and season with salt and pepper.
2. Preheat your Kaloric Maxx Air Fryer Oven to 400°F (200°C) using the Air Fry function.
3. Place the corn in the air fryer basket.
4. Air fry at 400°F (200°C) for 10-12 minutes, turning halfway through, until the corn is tender and lightly charred.
5. Serve hot, sprinkled with fresh chopped parsley and with lime wedges on the side.

NUTRITIONAL INFO (PER SERVING): Calories: 110 | Fat: 5g | Carbs: 17g | Protein: 3g

Kaloric Maxx Air Fryer Oven Functions Used: Air Fry

Tip: For extra flavor, sprinkle grated Parmesan cheese or chili powder over the cooked corn before serving.

AIR FRYER ROASTED BRUSSELS SPROUTS

Prep: 10 mins | Cook: 15 mins | Serves: 4

INGREDIENTS:

- 1 lb (450g) Brussels sprouts, trimmed and halved / 450g Brussels sprouts, trimmed and halved
- 2 tablespoons olive oil / 30ml olive oil
- 2 cloves garlic, minced / 2 cloves garlic, minced
- Salt and pepper, to taste / Salt and pepper, to taste
- Balsamic glaze, for drizzling /
- Balsamic glaze, for drizzling

INSTRUCTIONS:

1. In a large bowl, toss the Brussels sprouts with olive oil, minced garlic, salt, and pepper until evenly coated.
2. Preheat your Kaloric Maxx Air Fryer Oven to 375°F (190°C) using the Air Fry function.
3. Transfer the seasoned Brussels sprouts to the air fryer basket.
4. Air fry at 375°F (190°C) for 12-15 minutes, shaking the basket halfway through, until the Brussels sprouts are tender and caramelized.
5. Drizzle with balsamic glaze before serving.

NUTRITIONAL INFO (PER SERVING): Calories: 100 | Fat: 7g | Carbs: 9g | Protein: 3g

Kaloric Maxx Air Fryer Oven Functions Used: Air Fry

Tip: For a sweet and tangy flavor, substitute honey or maple syrup for the balsamic glaze.

AIR FRYER HASSELBACK POTATOES

Prep: 10 mins | Cook: 35 mins | Serves: 4

INGREDIENTS:

- 4 large russet potatoes / 4 large russet potatoes
- 2 tablespoons olive oil / 30ml olive oil
- 2 cloves garlic, minced / 2 cloves garlic, minced
- Salt and pepper, to taste / Salt and pepper, to taste
- Grated cheese, chopped chives, and sour cream, for topping / Grated cheese, chopped chives, and sour cream, for topping

INSTRUCTIONS:

1. Scrub the potatoes clean and pat them dry with a paper towel.
2. Slice each potato crosswise at 1/8-inch intervals, cutting only 3/4 of the way through.
3. Brush olive oil over the potatoes, making sure to get in between the slices.
4. Season with minced garlic, salt, and pepper, getting the seasonings in between the slices.
5. Preheat your Kaloric Maxx Air Fryer Oven to 400°F (200°C) using the Air Fry function.
6. Place the seasoned potatoes in the air fryer basket.

7. Air fry at 400°F (200°C) for 30-35 minutes, until the potatoes are tender and crispy.
8. Top with grated cheese, chopped chives, and sour cream before serving.

NUTRITIONAL INFO (PER SERVING): Calories: 220 | Fat: 7g | Carbs: 35g | Protein: 5g

Kaloric Maxx Air Fryer Oven Functions Used: Air Fry

Tip: Place the potatoes on a wooden spoon when slicing to prevent cutting all the way through.

AIR FRYER ROASTED BEETS

Prep: 10 mins | Cook: 35 mins | Serves: 4

INGREDIENTS:

- 4 medium beets, peeled and cubed / 4 medium beets, peeled and cubed
- 2 tablespoons olive oil / 30ml olive oil
- 2 cloves garlic, minced / 2 cloves garlic, minced
- Salt and pepper, to taste / Salt and pepper, to taste
- Fresh thyme leaves, for garnish / Fresh thyme leaves, for garnish

INSTRUCTIONS:

1. In a large bowl, toss the cubed beets with olive oil, minced garlic, salt, and pepper until well coated.
2. Preheat your Kaloric Maxx Air Fryer Oven to 375°F (190°C) using the Air Fry function.
3. Transfer the seasoned beets to the air fryer basket.

4. Air fry at 375°F (190°C) for 30-35 minutes, shaking the basket halfway through, until the beets are tender and caramelized.
5. Garnish with fresh thyme leaves before serving.

NUTRITIONAL INFO (PER SERVING): Calories: 90 | Fat: 7g | Carbs: 7g | Protein: 1g

Kaloric Maxx Air Fryer Oven Functions Used: Air Fry

Tip: Wear gloves when handling beets to prevent staining your hands.

AIR FRYER BUTTERNUT SQUASH

Prep: 10 mins | Cook: 20 mins | Serves: 4

INGREDIENTS:

- 1 medium butternut squash, peeled, seeded, and cubed / 1 medium butternut squash, peeled, seeded, and cubed
- 2 tablespoons olive oil / 30ml olive oil
- 1 teaspoon smoked paprika / 1 teaspoon smoked paprika
- 1 teaspoon ground cinnamon / 1 teaspoon ground cinnamon
- Salt and pepper, to taste / Salt and pepper, to taste
- Honey, for drizzling / Honey, for drizzling

INSTRUCTIONS:

1. In a large bowl, toss the cubed butternut squash with olive oil, smoked paprika, ground cinnamon, salt, and pepper until evenly coated.
2. Preheat your Kaloric Maxx Air Fryer Oven to 400°F (200°C) using the Air Fry function.
3. Transfer the seasoned butternut squash to the air fryer basket.
4. Air fry at 400°F (200°C) for 18-20 minutes, shaking the basket halfway through, until the squash is tender and caramelized.
5. Drizzle with honey before serving.

NUTRITIONAL INFO (PER SERVING): Calories: 100 | Fat: 7g | Carbs: 10g | Protein: 1g

Kaloric Maxx Air Fryer Oven Functions Used: Air Fry

Tip: To save time, use pre-cut butternut squash from the grocery store.

AIR FRYER ROASTED GARLIC

Prep: 5 mins | Cook: 30 mins | Serves: 4

INGREDIENTS:

- 4 whole heads of garlic / 4 whole heads of garlic
- 1 tablespoon olive oil / 15ml olive oil
- Salt and pepper, to taste / Salt and pepper, to taste

INSTRUCTIONS:

1. Slice off the top quarter of each head of garlic to expose the cloves.
2. Drizzle olive oil over the exposed cloves and season with salt and pepper.
3. Wrap each head of garlic in aluminum foil.
4. Preheat your Kaloric Maxx Air Fryer Oven to 375°F (190°C) using the Roast function.
5. Place the wrapped garlic heads directly on the oven rack.
6. Roast for 25-30 minutes, until the cloves are soft and caramelized.
7. Allow to cool slightly before squeezing out the roasted garlic cloves.

NUTRITIONAL INFO (PER SERVING): Calories: 50 | Fat: 4g | Carbs: 3g | Protein: 1g

Kaloric Maxx Air Fryer Oven Functions Used: Roast

Tip: Use roasted garlic

as a spread for bread, mixed into mashed potatoes, or stirred into sauces for extra flavor.

PIZZA AND BREAD

AIR FRYER PIZZA

Prep: 15 mins | Cook: 12 mins | Serves: 2

INGREDIENTS:

- 1 pre-made pizza dough / 1 pre-made pizza dough
- 1/2 cup marinara sauce / 120ml marinara sauce
- 1 cup shredded mozzarella cheese / 100g shredded mozzarella cheese
- Your favorite pizza toppings / Your favorite pizza toppings

INSTRUCTIONS:

1. Roll out the pizza dough on a lightly floured surface until it's your desired thickness.
2. Preheat your Kaloric Maxx Air Fryer Oven to 375°F (190°C) using the Air Fry function.
3. Place the rolled-out pizza dough on the air fryer tray.
4. Spread marinara sauce over the dough, leaving a border around the edges.
5. Sprinkle shredded mozzarella cheese over the sauce and add your favorite toppings.
6. Air fry at 375°F (190°C) for 10-12 minutes, until the crust is golden and the cheese is bubbly.
7. Slice and serve hot.

NUTRITIONAL INFO (PER SERVING): Calories: 350 | Fat: 12g | Carbs: 45g | Protein: 15g

Kaloric Maxx Air Fryer Oven Functions Used: Air Fry

Tip: Experiment with different toppings like pepperoni, mushrooms, bell peppers, and onions.

AIR FRYER GARLIC KNOTS

Prep: 10 mins | Cook: 8 mins | Serves: 4

INGREDIENTS:

- 1 lb pizza dough / 450g pizza dough
- 2 tablespoons melted butter / 30g melted butter
- 2 cloves garlic, minced / 2 cloves garlic, minced
- 1 tablespoon chopped fresh parsley / 15g chopped fresh parsley
- Salt, to taste / Salt, to taste

INSTRUCTIONS:

1. Divide the pizza dough into 12 equal pieces and roll each into a rope.
2. Tie each rope into a knot and place on a parchment-lined tray.
3. Preheat your Kaloric Maxx Air Fryer Oven to 375°F (190°C) using the Air Fry function.
4. In a small bowl, mix melted butter, minced garlic, chopped parsley, and salt.
5. Brush the garlic butter mixture over the knots.
6. Air fry at 375°F (190°C) for 6-8 minutes, until golden brown.
7. Serve warm.

NUTRITIONAL INFO (PER SERVING): Calories: 180 | Fat: 6g | Carbs: 28g | Protein: 5g

Kaloric Maxx Air Fryer Oven Functions Used: Air Fry

Tip: Serve garlic knots with marinara sauce for dipping.

AIR FRYER CALZONES

Prep: 15 mins | Cook: 12 mins | Serves: 2

INGREDIENTS:

- 1 lb pizza dough / 450g pizza dough
- 1/2 cup ricotta cheese / 120g ricotta cheese
- 1 cup shredded mozzarella cheese / 100g shredded mozzarella cheese
- 1/4 cup marinara sauce / 60ml marinara sauce
- Your favorite calzone fillings (e.g., pepperoni, cooked sausage, sautéed vegetables) / Your favorite calzone fillings

INSTRUCTIONS:

1. Divide the pizza dough into 2 equal pieces and roll each into a circle.
2. Spread marinara sauce on one half of each circle, leaving a border around the edge.
3. Top with ricotta cheese, shredded mozzarella cheese, and your favorite fillings.
4. Fold the dough over the fillings and crimp the edges to seal.
5. Preheat your Kaloric Maxx Air Fryer Oven to 375°F (190°C) using the Air Fry function.
6. Place the calzones on the air fryer tray.
7. Air fry at 375°F (190°C) for 10-12 minutes, until golden brown.
8. Serve hot.

NUTRITIONAL INFO (PER SERVING): Calories: 450 | Fat: 18g | Carbs: 50g | Protein: 20g

Kaloric Maxx Air Fryer Oven Functions Used: Air Fry

Tip: Customize your calzones with your favorite pizza toppings for a delicious meal.

AIR FRYER BREADSTICKS

Prep: 15 mins | Cook: 10 mins | Serves: 4

INGREDIENTS:

- 1 lb pizza dough / 450g pizza dough
- 2 tablespoons olive oil / 30ml olive oil
- 2 cloves garlic, minced / 2 cloves garlic, minced
- 1 teaspoon dried oregano / 1 teaspoon dried oregano
- 1/4 cup grated Parmesan cheese / 25g grated Parmesan cheese
- Salt, to taste / Salt, to taste

INSTRUCTIONS:

1. Roll out the pizza dough into a rectangle shape on a floured surface.
2. Preheat your Kaloric Maxx Air Fryer Oven to 375°F (190°C) using the Air Fry function.
3. Cut the dough into breadstick-sized strips.
4. In a small bowl, mix olive oil, minced garlic, dried oregano, and salt.
5. Brush the olive oil mixture over the breadsticks and sprinkle with grated Parmesan cheese.
6. Place the breadsticks on the air fryer tray.
7. Air fry at 375°F (190°C) for 8-10 minutes, until golden brown.
8. Serve warm with marinara sauce for dipping.

NUTRITIONAL INFO (PER SERVING): Calories: 220 | Fat: 8g | Carbs: 32g | Protein: 6g

Kaloric Maxx Air Fryer Oven Functions Used: Air Fry

Tip: Experiment with different seasonings like garlic powder, onion powder, or Italian seasoning.

AIR FRYER STROMBOLI

Prep: 20 mins | Cook: 15 mins | Serves: 4

INGREDIENTS:

- 1 lb pizza dough / 450g pizza dough
- 1/2 cup marinara sauce / 120ml marinara sauce
- 8 slices ham / 8 slices ham
- 8 slices salami / 8 slices salami
- 1 cup shredded mozzarella cheese / 100g shredded mozzarella cheese
- 1/4 cup sliced black olives / 25g sliced black olives

INSTRUCTIONS:

1. Roll out the pizza dough into a rectangle shape on a floured surface.
2. Spread marinara sauce over the dough, leaving a border around the edges.
3. Layer ham, salami, shredded mozzarella cheese, and sliced black olives on top of the sauce.
4. Roll up the dough tightly and seal the edges.
5. Preheat your Kaloric Maxx Air Fryer Oven to 375°F (190°C) using the Air Fry function.
6. Place the stromboli on the air fryer tray.
7. Air fry at 375°F (190°C) for 12-15 minutes, until golden brown and crispy.
8. Let it cool for a few minutes before slicing.
9. Serve warm with marinara sauce for dipping.

NUTRITIONAL INFO (PER SERVING): Calories: 380 | Fat: 15g | Carbs: 45g | Protein: 18g

Kaloric Maxx Air Fryer Oven Functions Used: Air Fry

Tip: Customize your stromboli with your favorite fillings like peppers, onions, or mushrooms.

AIR FRYER BAGELS

Prep: 20 mins | Cook: 12 mins | Serves: 4

INGREDIENTS:

- 1 lb pizza dough / 450g pizza dough
- 1 egg, beaten / 1 egg, beaten
- Everything bagel seasoning / Everything bagel seasoning

INSTRUCTIONS:

1. Divide the pizza dough into 4 equal pieces and shape each into a ball.
2. Poke a hole in the center of each ball and stretch to form a bagel shape.
3. Preheat your Kaloric Maxx Air Fryer Oven to 375°F (190°C) using the Air Fry function.
4. Brush the beaten egg over the tops of the bagels and sprinkle with everything bagel seasoning.
5. Place the bagels on the air fryer tray.
6. Air fry at 375°F (190°C) for 10-12 minutes, until golden brown.
7. Let them cool before slicing and serving.

NUTRITIONAL INFO (PER SERVING): Calories: 280 | Fat: 6g | Carbs: 48g | Protein: 9g

Kaloric Maxx Air Fryer Oven Functions Used: Air Fry

Tip: Enjoy your bagels toasted with cream cheese or your favorite spread.

AIR FRYER NAAN BREAD

Prep: 15 mins | Cook: 10 mins | Serves: 4

INGREDIENTS:

- 2 cups all-purpose flour / 250g all-purpose flour
- 1 teaspoon baking powder / 1 teaspoon baking powder
- 1/2 teaspoon salt / 1/2 teaspoon salt
- 1/4 cup plain yogurt / 60g plain yogurt
- 2 tablespoons olive oil / 30ml olive oil
- 1/2 cup warm water / 120ml warm water
- 2 tablespoons melted butter / 30g melted butter
- Chopped fresh cilantro, for garnish / Chopped fresh cilantro, for garnish

INSTRUCTIONS:

1. In a large bowl, mix together flour, baking powder, and salt.
2. Add yogurt, olive oil, and warm water to the flour mixture.
3. Knead the dough until smooth and elastic, adding more flour if necessary.
4. Cover the dough with a damp cloth and let it rest for 10 minutes.
5. Divide the dough into 4 equal portions and roll each into a ball.
6. Preheat your Kaloric Maxx Air Fryer Oven to 400°F (200°C) using the Air Fry function.
7. Roll out each ball of dough into a teardrop shape.

8. Brush one side of each naan with melted butter.

9. Place the naan, buttered side down, on the air fryer tray.

10. Air fry at 400°F (200°C) for 4-5 minutes, until puffed and golden brown.

11. Brush the cooked naan with more melted butter and sprinkle with chopped cilantro.

12. Serve warm as a side or with your favorite curry.

NUTRITIONAL INFO (PER SERVING): Calories: 280 | Fat: 9g | Carbs: 42g | Protein: 6g

Kaloric Maxx Air Fryer Oven Functions Used: Air Fry

Tip: Customize your naan bread by adding minced garlic or nigella seeds to the dough for extra flavor.

AIR FRYER PITA BREAD

Prep: 15 mins | Cook: 10 mins | Serves: 4

INGREDIENTS:

- 2 cups all-purpose flour / 250g all-purpose flour
- 1 teaspoon salt / 1 teaspoon salt
- 1 teaspoon sugar / 1 teaspoon sugar
- 1 teaspoon instant yeast / 1 teaspoon instant yeast
- 3/4 cup warm water / 180ml warm water
- 1 tablespoon olive oil / 15ml olive oil

INSTRUCTIONS:

1. In a large bowl, mix together flour, salt, sugar, and instant yeast.

2. Add warm water and olive oil to the flour mixture.

3. Knead the dough until smooth and elastic, adding more flour if necessary.

4. Cover the dough with a damp cloth and let it rest for 10 minutes.

5. Preheat your Kaloric Maxx Air Fryer Oven to 375°F (190°C) using the Air Fry function.

6. Divide the dough into 4 equal portions and roll each into a ball.

7. Roll out each ball of dough into a circle.

8. Place the pita dough circles on the air fryer tray.

9. Air fry at 375°F (190°C) for 8-10 minutes, until puffed and lightly golden.

10. Serve warm with hummus or use for sandwiches.

NUTRITIONAL INFO (PER SERVING): Calories: 220 | Fat: 5g | Carbs: 38g | Protein: 6g

Kaloric Maxx Air Fryer Oven Functions Used: Air Fry

Tip: For best results, let the dough rest for a few minutes before air frying to allow it to rise slightly.

AIR FRYER FOCACCIA

Prep: 20 mins | Cook: 15 mins | Serves: 4

INGREDIENTS:

- 2 cups all-purpose flour / 250g all-purpose flour
- 1 teaspoon salt / 1 teaspoon salt
- 1 teaspoon sugar / 1 teaspoon sugar
- 1 teaspoon instant yeast / 1 teaspoon instant yeast
- 3/4 cup warm water / 180ml warm water
- 1 tablespoon olive oil / 15ml olive oil
- 2 tablespoons olive oil, for brushing / 30ml olive oil, for brushing
- 1 teaspoon dried rosemary / 1 teaspoon dried rosemary
- Sea salt, for sprinkling / Sea salt, for sprinkling

INSTRUCTIONS:

1. In a large bowl, mix together flour, salt, sugar, and instant yeast.
2. Add warm water and olive oil to the flour mixture.
3. Knead the dough until smooth and elastic, adding more flour if necessary.
4. Cover the dough with a damp cloth and let it rest for 10 minutes.
5. Preheat your Kaloric Maxx Air Fryer Oven to 375°F (190°C) using the Air Fry function.
6. Roll out the dough into a rectangle shape.
7. Place the dough on the air fryer tray and brush with olive oil.
8. Sprinkle dried rosemary and sea salt over the top.
9. Use your fingers to create dimples in the dough.
10. Air fry at 375°F (190°C) for 12-15 minutes, until golden brown.
11. Serve warm as a side or with your favorite dip.

NUTRITIONAL INFO (PER SERVING): Calories: 250 | Fat: 10g | Carbs: 35g | Protein: 6g

Kaloric Maxx Air Fryer Oven Functions Used: Air Fry

Tip: Add toppings like sliced olives, cherry tomatoes, or caramelized onions for extra flavor.

AIR FRYER BAGUETTES

Prep: 20 mins | Cook: 15 mins | Serves: 4

INGREDIENTS:

- 2 cups all-purpose flour / 250g all-purpose flour
- 1 teaspoon salt / 1 teaspoon salt
- 1 teaspoon sugar / 1 teaspoon sugar
- 1 teaspoon instant yeast / 1 teaspoon instant yeast
- 3/4 cup warm water / 180ml warm water

INSTRUCTIONS:

1. In a large bowl, mix together flour, salt, sugar, and instant yeast.
2. Add warm water to the flour mixture.
3. Knead the dough until smooth and elastic, adding more flour if necessary.
4. Cover the dough with a damp cloth and let it rest for 10 minutes.
5. Preheat your Kaloric Maxx Air Fryer Oven to 375°F (190°C) using the Air Fry function.
6. Divide the dough into 4 equal portions and shape each into a baguette.
7. Place the baguettes on the air fryer tray and slash the tops with a sharp knife.
8. Air fry at 375°F (190°C) for 12-15 minutes, until golden brown.
9. Serve warm with butter or as a sandwich base.

NUTRITIONAL INFO (PER SERVING): Calories: 200 | Fat: 1g | Carbs: 40g | Protein: 6g

Kaloric Maxx Air Fryer Oven Functions Used: Air Fry

Tip: For a crispy crust, brush the baguettes with water before air frying.

AIR FRYER CINNAMON ROLLS

Prep: 20 mins | Cook: 12 mins | Serves: 4

INGREDIENTS:

- 1 lb pizza dough / 450g pizza dough
- 1/4 cup melted butter / 60g melted butter
- 1/4 cup brown sugar / 50g brown sugar
- 1 tablespoon ground cinnamon / 1 tablespoon ground cinnamon
- 1/2 cup powdered sugar / 60g powdered sugar
- 1 tablespoon milk / 15ml milk

INSTRUCTIONS:

1. Roll out the pizza dough into a rectangle shape on a floured surface.
2. Brush melted butter over the dough.
3. In a small bowl, mix brown sugar and ground cinnamon.
4. Sprinkle the cinnamon sugar mixture evenly over the buttered dough.
5. Roll up the dough tightly and cut into 8 equal pieces.
6. Preheat your Kaloric Maxx Air Fryer Oven to 375°F (190°C) using the Air Fry function.
7. Place the cinnamon rolls on the air fryer tray.
8. Air fry at 375°F (190°C) for 10-12 minutes, until golden brown.

9. In a small bowl, mix powdered sugar and milk to make the icing.
10. Drizzle the icing over the warm cinnamon rolls before serving.

NUTRITIONAL INFO (PER SERVING): Calories: 300 | Fat: 10g | Carbs: 50g | Protein: 5g

Kaloric Maxx Air Fryer Oven Functions Used: Air Fry

Tip: Add a handful of raisins or chopped nuts to the filling for added texture and flavor.

8. Air fry at 375°F (190°C) for 8-10 minutes, until golden brown.
9. Serve warm with mustard or cheese sauce.

NUTRITIONAL INFO (PER SERVING): Calories: 250 | Fat: 4g | Carbs: 48g | Protein: 8g

Kaloric Maxx Air Fryer Oven Functions Used: Air Fry

Tip: For sweet pretzels, sprinkle with cinnamon sugar instead of salt.

AIR FRYER PRETZELS

Prep: 20 mins | Cook: 10 mins | Serves: 4

INGREDIENTS:

- 1 lb pizza dough / 450g pizza dough
- 1/4 cup baking soda / 60g baking soda
- 1 egg, beaten / 1 egg, beaten
- Coarse salt, for sprinkling / Coarse salt, for sprinkling

INSTRUCTIONS:

1. Divide the pizza dough into 4 equal pieces and roll each into a rope.
2. Shape each rope into a pretzel.
3. Bring a pot of water to a boil and add baking soda.
4. Boil each pretzel for 30 seconds, then drain on a paper towel.
5. Preheat your Kaloric Maxx Air Fryer Oven to 375°F (190°C) using the Air Fry function.
6. Brush the pretzels with beaten egg and sprinkle with coarse salt.
7. Place the pretzels on the air fryer tray.

AIR FRYER GARLIC BREAD

Prep: 10 mins | Cook: 8 mins | Serves: 4

INGREDIENTS:

- 1 baguette / 1 baguette
- 1/4 cup softened butter / 60g softened butter
- 2 cloves garlic, minced / 2 cloves garlic, minced
- 1 tablespoon chopped fresh parsley / 15g chopped fresh parsley
- Salt, to taste / Salt, to taste

INSTRUCTIONS:

1. Slice the baguette in half lengthwise.
2. In a small bowl, mix softened butter, minced garlic, chopped parsley, and salt.
3. Spread the garlic butter mixture evenly
1. over the cut sides of the baguette.
4. Preheat your Kaloric Maxx Air Fryer Oven to 375°F (190°C) using the Air Fry function.
5. Place the baguette halves on the air fryer tray.
6. Air fry at 375°F (190°C) for 6-8 minutes, until golden and crispy.
7. Serve warm as a side or appetizer.

NUTRITIONAL INFO (PER SERVING): Calories: 200 | Fat: 10g | Carbs: 25g | Protein: 4g

Kaloric Maxx Air Fryer Oven Functions Used: Air Fry

Tip: Add grated Parmesan cheese on top for an extra cheesy garlic bread.

AIR FRYER DINNER ROLLS

Prep: 20 mins | Cook: 12 mins | Serves: 4

INGREDIENTS:

- 2 cups all-purpose flour / 250g all-purpose flour
- 1 teaspoon salt / 1 teaspoon salt
- 1 tablespoon sugar / 1 tablespoon sugar
- 1 teaspoon instant yeast / 1 teaspoon instant yeast
- 3/4 cup warm milk / 180ml warm milk
- 2 tablespoons melted butter / 30g melted butter

INSTRUCTIONS:

1. In a large bowl, mix together flour, salt, sugar, and instant yeast.
2. Add warm milk and melted butter to the flour mixture.
3. Knead the dough until smooth and elastic, adding more flour if necessary.
4. Cover the dough with a damp cloth and let it rest for 10 minutes.
5. Preheat your Kaloric Maxx Air Fryer Oven to 375°F (190°C) using the Air Fry function.
6. Divide the dough into 8 equal portions and shape each into a ball.
7. Place the dough balls on the air fryer tray.
8. Air fry at 375°F (190°C) for 10-12 minutes, until golden brown.
9. Serve warm with butter.

NUTRITIONAL INFO (PER SERVING): Calories: 150 | Fat: 4g | Carbs: 25g | Protein: 4g

Kaloric Maxx Air Fryer Oven Functions Used: Air Fry

Tip: Brush the tops of the rolls with melted butter after baking for a shiny finish.

AIR FRYER FLATBREAD

Prep: 15 mins | Cook: 8 mins | Serves: 4

INGREDIENTS:

- 2 cups all-purpose flour / 250g all-purpose flour
- 1 teaspoon salt / 1 teaspoon salt
- 1/2 teaspoon baking powder / 1/2 teaspoon baking powder
- 1/4 cup plain yogurt / 60g plain yogurt
- 1/2 cup warm water / 120ml warm water
- 2 tablespoons olive oil / 30ml olive oil

INSTRUCTIONS:

1. In a large bowl, mix together flour, salt, and baking powder.
2. Add yogurt, warm water, and olive oil to the flour mixture.
3. Knead the dough until smooth and elastic, adding more flour if necessary.
4. Cover the dough with a damp cloth and let it rest for 10 minutes.
5. Preheat your Kaloric Maxx Air Fryer Oven to 375°F (190°C) using the Air Fry function.
6. Divide the dough into 4 equal portions and roll each into a circle.
7. Place the flatbreads on the air fryer tray.
8. Air fry at 375°F (190°C) for 6-8 minutes, until golden brown.
9. Serve warm with your favorite toppings or as a side.

NUTRITIONAL INFO (PER SERVING): Calories: 220 | Fat: 6g | Carbs: 35g | Protein: 5g

Kaloric Maxx Air Fryer Oven Functions Used: Air Fry

Tip: Use flatbreads as a base for quick pizzas or fold them into wraps.

DESSERTS

AIR FRYER CHOCOLATE LAVA CAKES

Prep: 15 mins | Cook: 10 mins | Serves: 4

INGREDIENTS:

- 4 ounces semisweet chocolate, chopped / 115g semisweet chocolate, chopped
- 1/2 cup unsalted butter / 115g unsalted butter
- 1/2 cup powdered sugar / 60g powdered sugar
- 2 eggs + 2 egg yolks / 2 eggs + 2 egg yolks
- 1/3 cup all-purpose flour / 40g all-purpose flour
- Pinch of salt / Pinch of salt

INSTRUCTIONS:

1. In a microwave-safe bowl, melt chocolate and butter together.
2. Stir in powdered sugar until smooth.
3. Add eggs and egg yolks, one at a time, mixing well after each addition.
4. Fold in flour and salt until just combined.
5. Preheat your Kaloric Maxx Air Fryer Oven to 375°F (190°C) using the Air Fry function.
6. Grease four ramekins and pour in the batter.
7. Place the ramekins in the air fryer basket.
8. Air fry at 375°F (190°C) for 8-10 minutes, until the edges are set but the centers are still soft.
9. Serve immediately, topped with ice cream if desired.

NUTRITIONAL INFO (PER SERVING): Calories: 380 | Fat: 28g | Carbs: 29g | Protein: 6g

Kaloric Maxx Air Fryer Oven Functions Used: Air Fry

Tip: Be careful not to overbake the lava cakes to maintain the gooey center.

AIR FRYER BAKED APPLES

Prep: 10 mins | Cook: 20 mins | Serves: 4

INGREDIENTS:

- 4 large apples, cored / 4 large apples, cored
- 1/4 cup brown sugar / 50g brown sugar
- 1 teaspoon ground cinnamon / 1 teaspoon ground cinnamon
- 1/4 cup chopped pecans / 30g chopped pecans
- 2 tablespoons unsalted butter, melted / 30g unsalted butter, melted
- Vanilla ice cream, for serving / Vanilla ice cream, for serving

INSTRUCTIONS:

1. In a bowl, mix brown sugar, cinnamon, chopped pecans, and melted butter.
2. Stuff each cored apple with the sugar mixture.

3. Preheat your Kaloric Maxx Air Fryer Oven to 350°F (175°C) using the Air Fry function.
4. Place the stuffed apples in the air fryer basket.
5. Air fry at 350°F (175°C) for 18-20 minutes, until tender.
6. Serve warm, topped with a scoop of vanilla ice cream.

Nutritional Info (per serving): Calories: 220 | Fat: 10g | Carbs: 35g | Protein: 2g

Kaloric Maxx Air Fryer Oven Functions Used: Air Fry

Tip: Adjust the sweetness according to your preference by adding more or less brown sugar.

AIR FRYER CHURROS

Prep: 15 mins | Cook: 10 mins | Serves: 4

INGREDIENTS:

- 1 cup water / 240ml water
- 1/2 cup unsalted butter / 115g unsalted butter
- 1 tablespoon granulated sugar / 15g granulated sugar
- 1/4 teaspoon salt / 1/4 teaspoon salt
- 1 cup all-purpose flour / 120g all-purpose flour
- 2 eggs / 2 eggs
- 1/2 teaspoon vanilla extract / 1/2 teaspoon vanilla extract
- 1/4 cup granulated sugar, for coating / 50g granulated sugar, for coating
- 1 teaspoon ground cinnamon / 1 teaspoon ground cinnamon

INSTRUCTIONS:

1. In a saucepan, bring water, butter, sugar, and salt to a boil.
2. Reduce heat and stir in flour until the mixture forms a ball.
3. Transfer the dough to a mixing bowl and let it cool for a few minutes.
4. Add eggs, one at a time, and vanilla extract, beating well after each addition.
5. Preheat your Kaloric Maxx Air Fryer Oven to 375°F (190°C) using the Air Fry function.
6. Transfer the dough to a piping bag fitted with a star tip.
7. Pipe strips of dough onto the air fryer basket.
8. Air fry at 375°F (190°C) for 8-10 minutes, until golden brown and crispy.
9. Mix sugar and cinnamon in a shallow dish.
10. Roll the hot churros in the cinnamon sugar mixture.
11. Serve immediately with chocolate sauce or dulce de leche for dipping.

Nutritional Info (per serving): Calories: 320 | Fat: 18g | Carbs: 38g | Protein: 5g

Kaloric Maxx Air Fryer Oven Functions Used: Air Fry

Tip: Pipe the churro dough directly into the air fryer basket for easy cleanup.

AIR FRYER DONUTS

Prep: 15 mins | Cook: 10 mins | Serves: 4

INGREDIENTS:

- 1 can refrigerated biscuit dough / 1 can refrigerated biscuit dough
- 1/4 cup granulated sugar / 50g granulated sugar
- 1 tablespoon ground cinnamon / 15g ground cinnamon
- 1/4 cup unsalted butter, melted / 60g unsalted butter, melted

INSTRUCTIONS:

1. Open the can of biscuit dough and separate the biscuits.
2. Use a small round cutter to cut out the centers of each biscuit to make donuts.
3. Preheat your Kaloric Maxx Air Fryer Oven to 350°F (175°C) using the Air Fry function.
4. Place the donuts in the air fryer basket.
5. Air fry at 350°F (175°C) for 5 minutes, then flip the donuts over.
6. Continue air frying for another 3-5 minutes, until golden brown and cooked through.
7. Mix sugar and cinnamon in a shallow dish.
8. Brush the hot donuts with melted butter, then dip them in the cinnamon sugar mixture.
9. Serve warm with a glass of cold milk.

NUTRITIONAL INFO (PER SERVING): Calories: 280 | Fat: 14g | Carbs: 35g | Protein: 3g

Kaloric Maxx Air Fryer Oven Functions Used: Air Fry

Tip: Use the donut holes to make mini donuts or save them for another use.

AIR FRYER CINNAMON SUGAR PRETZEL BITES

Prep: 20 mins | Cook: 8 mins | Serves: 4

INGREDIENTS:

- 1 cup warm water / 240ml warm water
- 1 tablespoon sugar / 15g sugar
- 2 teaspoons active dry yeast / 2 teaspoons active dry yeast
- 3 cups all-purpose flour / 375g all-purpose flour
- 1 teaspoon salt / 1 teaspoon salt
- 1/4 cup baking soda / 60g baking soda
- 1/2 cup granulated sugar / 100g granulated sugar
- 1 tablespoon ground cinnamon / 15g ground cinnamon
- 4 tablespoons unsalted butter, melted / 60g unsalted butter, melted

INSTRUCTIONS:

1. In a bowl, combine warm water, sugar, and yeast. Let it sit until foamy, about 5 minutes.
2. Add flour and salt to the yeast mixture, and knead until a smooth dough forms.
3. Cover the dough and let it rise for 10 minutes.
4. Preheat your Kaloric Maxx Air Fryer Oven to 375°F (190°C) using the Air Fry function.

5. Divide the dough into small pieces and roll each into a ball.
6. Bring a pot of water to a boil and add baking soda.
7. Boil the dough balls for 30 seconds, then remove and drain.
8. Place the dough balls in the air fryer basket.
9. Air fry at 375°F (190°C) for 6-8 minutes, until golden brown.
10. Mix sugar and cinnamon in a shallow dish.
11. Brush the hot pretzel bites with melted butter, then roll them in the cinnamon sugar mixture.
12. Serve warm with your favorite dipping sauce.

NUTRITIONAL INFO (PER SERVING): Calories: 320 | Fat: 10g | Carbs: 52g | Protein: 6g

Kaloric Maxx Air Fryer Oven Functions Used: Air Fry

Tip: Serve with a sweet cream cheese dip for extra indulgence.

AIR FRYER CHOCOLATE CHIP COOKIES

Prep: 10 mins | Cook: 8 mins | Serves: 4

INGREDIENTS:

- 1/2 cup unsalted butter, softened / 115g unsalted butter, softened
- 1/2 cup brown sugar / 100g brown sugar
- 1/4 cup granulated sugar / 50g granulated sugar
- 1 egg / 1 egg
- 1 teaspoon vanilla extract / 1 teaspoon vanilla extract
- 1 1/4 cups all-purpose flour / 150g all-purpose flour
- 1/2 teaspoon baking soda / 1/2 teaspoon baking soda
- 1/4 teaspoon salt / 1/4 teaspoon salt
- 1 cup chocolate chips / 150g chocolate chips

INSTRUCTIONS:

1. In a large bowl, cream together butter, brown sugar, and granulated sugar.
2. Beat in the egg and vanilla extract.
3. Add flour, baking soda, and salt, mixing until just combined.
4. Fold in chocolate chips.
5. Preheat your Kaloric Maxx Air Fryer Oven to 350°F (175°C) using the Air Fry function.
6. Drop spoonfuls of dough onto the air fryer tray.
7. Air fry at 350°F (175°C) for 6-8 minutes, until golden brown.
8. Let cookies cool on a wire rack.
9. Serve with a glass of cold milk.

NUTRITIONAL INFO (PER SERVING): Calories: 260 | Fat: 14g | Carbs: 33g | Protein: 3g

Kaloric Maxx Air Fryer Oven Functions Used: Air Fry

Tip: Do not overfill the air fryer tray to ensure even cooking.

AIR FRYER BROWNIES

Prep: 10 mins | Cook: 20 mins | Serves: 4

INGREDIENTS:

- 1/2 cup unsalted butter / 115g unsalted butter
- 1 cup granulated sugar / 200g granulated sugar
- 2 eggs / 2 eggs
- 1 teaspoon vanilla extract / 1 teaspoon vanilla extract
- 1/3 cup cocoa powder / 40g cocoa powder
- 1/2 cup all-purpose flour / 60g all-purpose flour
- 1/4 teaspoon salt / 1/4 teaspoon salt
- 1/4 teaspoon baking powder / 1/4 teaspoon baking powder

INSTRUCTIONS:

1. In a microwave-safe bowl, melt the butter.
2. Stir in the sugar, eggs, and vanilla extract.
3. Add cocoa powder, flour, salt, and baking powder, mixing until well combined.
4. Preheat your Kaloric Maxx Air Fryer Oven to 325°F (160°C) using the Bake function.
5. Pour the batter into a greased baking dish that fits into the air fryer basket.
6. Bake at 325°F (160°C) for 15-20 minutes, until a toothpick inserted in the center comes out clean.
7. Let brownies cool before cutting into squares.
8. Serve with a scoop of vanilla ice cream.

NUTRITIONAL INFO (PER SERVING): Calories: 340 | Fat: 18g | Carbs: 45g | Protein: 4g

Kaloric Maxx Air Fryer Oven Functions Used: Bake

Tip: Add nuts or chocolate chips to the batter for extra texture.

AIR FRYER APPLE FRITTERS

Prep: 15 mins | Cook: 10 mins | Serves: 4

INGREDIENTS:

- 1 cup all-purpose flour / 120g all-purpose flour
- 1/4 cup granulated sugar / 50g granulated sugar
- 1 1/2 teaspoons baking powder / 1 1/2 teaspoons baking powder
- 1/2 teaspoon ground cinnamon / 1/2 teaspoon ground cinnamon
- 1/4 teaspoon salt / 1/4 teaspoon salt
- 1/3 cup milk / 80ml milk
- 1 egg / 1 egg
- 1 teaspoon vanilla extract / 1 teaspoon vanilla extract
- 1 large apple, peeled and chopped / 1 large apple, peeled and chopped
- 1/4 cup powdered sugar, for dusting / 30g powdered sugar, for dusting

INSTRUCTIONS:

1. In a large bowl, combine flour, granulated sugar, baking powder, cinnamon, and salt.
2. Whisk in milk, egg, and vanilla extract until smooth.
3. Fold in chopped apples.
4. Preheat your Kaloric Maxx Air Fryer Oven to 375°F (190°C) using the Air Fry function.
5. Drop spoonfuls of batter onto the air fryer tray.
6. Air fry at 375°F (190°C) for 8-10 minutes, until golden brown.
7. Dust with powdered sugar.
8. Serve warm with a drizzle of honey.

NUTRITIONAL INFO (PER SERVING): Calories: 240 | Fat: 8g | Carbs: 40g | Protein: 4g

Kaloric Maxx Air Fryer Oven Functions Used: Air Fry

Tip: Use different types of apples for varying flavors and textures.

AIR FRYER BANANA BREAD

Prep: 10 mins | Cook: 20 mins | Serves: 1 loaf

INGREDIENTS:

- 1 cup mashed ripe bananas / 240g mashed ripe bananas
- 1/2 cup granulated sugar / 100g granulated sugar
- 1/4 cup unsalted butter, melted / 60g unsalted butter, melted
- 1 egg / 1 egg
- 1 teaspoon vanilla extract / 1 teaspoon vanilla extract
- 1 1/2 cups all-purpose flour / 180g all-purpose flour
- 1 teaspoon baking powder / 1 teaspoon baking powder
- 1/2 teaspoon baking soda / 1/2 teaspoon baking soda
- 1/4 teaspoon salt / 1/4 teaspoon salt

INSTRUCTIONS:

1. In a large bowl, combine mashed bananas, sugar, melted butter, egg, and vanilla extract.
2. Add flour, baking powder, baking soda, and salt, mixing until just combined.
3. Preheat your Kaloric Maxx Air Fryer Oven to 325°F (160°C) using the Bake function.
4. Pour the batter into a greased loaf pan that fits into the air fryer basket.
5. Bake at 325°F (160°C) for 18-20 minutes, until a toothpick inserted in the center comes out clean.
6. Let the banana bread cool before slicing.
7. Serve with a smear of butter.

NUTRITIONAL INFO (PER SERVING): Calories: 250 | Fat: 8g | Carbs: 45g | Protein: 4g

Kaloric Maxx Air Fryer Oven Functions Used: Bake

Tip: Add nuts or chocolate chips to the batter for extra flavor.

AIR FRYER CHEESECAKE

Prep: 15 mins | Cook: 30 mins | Serves: 6

INGREDIENTS:

- 1 cup graham cracker crumbs / 120g graham cracker crumbs
- 1/4 cup unsalted butter, melted / 60g unsalted butter, melted
- 2 packages cream cheese, softened / 450g cream cheese, softened
- 1/2 cup granulated sugar / 100g granulated sugar
- 2 eggs / 2 eggs
- 1 teaspoon vanilla extract / 1 teaspoon vanilla extract

INSTRUCTIONS:

1. In a bowl, combine graham cracker crumbs and melted butter.
2. Press the mixture into the bottom of a springform pan.
3. In another bowl, beat cream cheese and sugar until smooth.
4. Add eggs one at a time, beating well after each addition.
5. Stir in vanilla extract.
6. Preheat your Kaloric Maxx Air Fryer Oven to 300°F (150°C) using the Bake function.
7. Pour the cheesecake batter over the crust.

8. Bake at 300°F (150°C) for 30 minutes, until the center is set.
9. Let the cheesecake cool, then refrigerate for at least 2 hours before serving.
10. Serve with your favorite fruit topping.

NUTRITIONAL INFO (PER SERVING): Calories: 450 | Fat: 33g | Carbs: 30g | Protein: 8g

Kaloric Maxx Air Fryer Oven Functions Used: Bake

Tip: Ensure the cream cheese is softened to avoid lumps in the batter.

AIR FRYER PINEAPPLE UPSIDE-DOWN CAKE

Prep: 15 mins | Cook: 20 mins | Serves: 4

INGREDIENTS:

- 1/4 cup unsalted butter / 60g unsalted butter
- 1/2 cup brown sugar / 100g brown sugar
- 4 pineapple rings / 4 pineapple rings
- 4 maraschino cherries / 4 maraschino cherries
- 1/2 cup granulated sugar / 100g granulated sugar
- 1/4 cup unsalted butter, softened / 60g unsalted butter, softened
- 1 egg / 1 egg
- 1 teaspoon vanilla extract / 1 teaspoon vanilla extract
- 1 cup all-purpose flour / 120g all-purpose flour
- 1 teaspoon baking powder / 1 teaspoon baking powder

- 1/4 teaspoon salt / 1/4 teaspoon salt
- 1/2 cup milk / 120ml milk

INSTRUCTIONS:

1. Melt 1/4 cup butter and stir in brown sugar. Spread the mixture in a cake pan.
2. Arrange pineapple rings and place a cherry in the center of each ring.
3. In a bowl, cream together granulated sugar and softened butter.
4. Add egg and vanilla extract, beating well.
5. In another bowl, combine flour, baking powder, and salt.
6. Add the dry ingredients to the creamed mixture alternately with milk, beating well.
7. Preheat your Kaloric Maxx Air Fryer Oven to 350°F (175°C) using the Bake function.
8. Pour the batter over the pineapple in the cake pan.
9. Bake at 350°F (175°C) for 20-25 minutes, until a toothpick inserted in the center comes out clean.
10. Let the cake cool for 5 minutes, then invert onto a plate.
11. Serve warm with a scoop of ice cream.

NUTRITIONAL INFO (PER SERVING): Calories: 380 | Fat: 18g | Carbs: 52g | Protein: 4g

Kaloric Maxx Air Fryer Oven Functions Used: Bake

Tip: Use fresh pineapple for a juicier cake.

AIR FRYER FRIED OREOS

Prep: 10 mins | Cook: 8 mins | Serves: 4

INGREDIENTS:

- 1 can refrigerated crescent roll dough / 1 can refrigerated crescent roll dough
- 16 Oreo cookies / 16 Oreo cookies
- Powdered sugar, for dusting / Powdered sugar, for dusting

INSTRUCTIONS:

1. Open the can of crescent roll dough and separate into triangles.
2. Wrap each Oreo cookie in a piece of dough, sealing the edges.
3. Preheat your Kaloric Maxx Air Fryer Oven to 350°F (175°C) using the Air Fry function.
4. Place the wrapped Oreos in the air fryer basket.
5. Air fry at 350°F (175°C) for 6-8 minutes, until golden brown.
6. Dust with powdered sugar.
7. Serve warm.

NUTRITIONAL INFO (PER SERVING): Calories: 200 | Fat: 10g | Carbs: 27g | Protein: 2g

Kaloric Maxx Air Fryer Oven Functions Used: Air Fry

Tip: Serve with a side of vanilla ice cream for a delicious treat.

AIR FRYER FRUIT CRISPS

Prep: 10 mins | Cook: 15 mins | Serves: 4

INGREDIENTS:

- 2 cups mixed berries (strawberries, blueberries, raspberries) / 300g mixed berries
- 1/4 cup granulated sugar / 50g granulated sugar
- 1/2 cup rolled oats / 50g rolled oats
- 1/4 cup all-purpose flour / 30g all-purpose flour
- 1/4 cup brown sugar / 50g brown sugar
- 1/4 cup unsalted butter, melted / 60g unsalted butter, melted

INSTRUCTIONS:

1. Preheat your Kaloric Maxx Air Fryer Oven to 350°F (175°C) using the Bake function.
2. In a bowl, toss mixed berries with granulated sugar.
3. Divide the berries among four ramekins.
4. In another bowl, combine rolled oats, flour, brown sugar, and melted butter to make the topping.
5. Sprinkle the topping over the berries in each ramekin.
6. Place the ramekins in the air fryer basket.
7. Bake at 350°F (175°C) for 12-15 minutes, until the topping is golden brown.
8. Serve warm with a scoop of vanilla ice cream.

NUTRITIONAL INFO (PER SERVING): Calories: 260 | Fat: 10g | Carbs: 42g | Protein: 3g

Kaloric Maxx Air Fryer Oven Functions Used: Bake

Tip: Use any combination of fruits you like for the crisps.

AIR FRYER CANNOLI

Prep: 15 mins | Cook: 10 mins | Serves: 4

INGREDIENTS:

- 8 cannoli shells / 8 cannoli shells
- 1 cup ricotta cheese / 240g ricotta cheese
- 1/2 cup powdered sugar / 60g powdered sugar
- 1/2 teaspoon vanilla extract / 1/2 teaspoon vanilla extract
- 1/4 cup mini chocolate chips / 40g mini chocolate chips
- Powdered sugar, for dusting / Powdered sugar, for dusting

INSTRUCTIONS:

1. In a bowl, mix ricotta cheese, powdered sugar, and vanilla extract until smooth.
2. Fold in mini chocolate chips.
3. Preheat your Kaloric Maxx Air Fryer Oven to 350°F (175°C) using the Air Fry function.
4. Place the cannoli shells in the air fryer basket.
5. Air fry at 350°F (175°C) for 5 minutes, until crispy.
6. Let the shells cool completely.
7. Pipe the ricotta mixture into the cooled cannoli shells.
8. Dust with powdered sugar.
9. Serve immediately.

NUTRITIONAL INFO (PER SERVING): Calories: 250 | Fat: 14g | Carbs: 28g | Protein: 6g

Kaloric Maxx Air Fryer Oven Functions Used: Air Fry

Tip: Ensure the ricotta cheese is well-drained to avoid a runny filling.

AIR FRYER BREAD PUDDING

Prep: 10 mins | Cook: 20 mins | Serves: 4

INGREDIENTS:

- 4 cups cubed bread / 240g cubed bread
- 2 cups milk / 480ml milk
- 1/2 cup granulated sugar / 100g granulated sugar
- 2 eggs / 2 eggs
- 1 teaspoon vanilla extract / 1 teaspoon vanilla extract
- 1/2 teaspoon ground cinnamon / 1/2 teaspoon ground cinnamon
- 1/4 cup raisins (optional) / 30g raisins (optional)

INSTRUCTIONS:

1. In a bowl, whisk together milk, sugar, eggs, vanilla extract, and ground cinnamon.
2. Add cubed bread and raisins (if using), stirring to combine.
3. Preheat your Kaloric Maxx Air Fryer Oven to 325°F (160°C) using the Bake function.
4. Pour the mixture into a baking dish that fits into the air fryer basket.
5. Bake at 325°F (160°C) for 20-25 minutes, until the pudding is set and golden.
6. Let it cool slightly before serving.
7. Serve warm with a drizzle of caramel sauce.

NUTRITIONAL INFO (PER SERVING): Calories: 300 | Fat: 8g | Carbs: 45g | Protein: 8g

Kaloric Maxx Air Fryer Oven Functions Used: Bake

Tip: Use stale bread for the best texture in bread pudding.

ROTISSERIE AND ROASTING

PERFECTLY JUICY AIR FRYER ROTISSERIE CHICKEN

Prep: 15 mins | Cook: 1 hour 30 mins | Serves: 4

INGREDIENTS:

- 1 whole chicken, about 3-4 lbs / 1.4-1.8 kg
- 2 tablespoons olive oil / 30ml olive oil
- 2 teaspoons paprika / 2 teaspoons paprika
- 1 teaspoon garlic powder / 1 teaspoon garlic powder
- 1 teaspoon onion powder / 1 teaspoon onion powder
- 1 teaspoon dried thyme / 1 teaspoon dried thyme
- 1 teaspoon dried rosemary / 1 teaspoon dried rosemary
- Salt and pepper to taste / Salt and pepper to taste

INSTRUCTIONS:

1. In a small bowl, mix together olive oil, paprika, garlic powder, onion powder, thyme, rosemary, salt, and pepper to form a paste.
2. Pat the chicken dry with paper towels and rub the spice paste all over the chicken, including under the skin.
3. Preheat your Kaloric Maxx Air Fryer Oven to 375°F (190°C) using the Rotisserie function.
4. Skewer the chicken onto the rotisserie spit, securing it tightly with the forks.
5. Place the spit into the air fryer oven and cook for 1 hour 30 minutes, or until the internal temperature of the chicken reaches 165°F (75°C).
6. Let the chicken rest for 10 minutes before carving.
7. Carve the chicken and serve hot.

NUTRITIONAL INFO (PER SERVING): Calories: 350 | Fat: 20g | Carbs: 1g | Protein: 38g

Kaloric Maxx Air Fryer Oven Functions Used: Rotisserie

Tip: For extra crispy skin, pat the chicken dry with paper towels before applying the spice rub.

SUCCULENT AIR FRYER ROASTED WHOLE TURKEY

Prep: 20 mins | Cook: 3 hours | Serves: 8

INGREDIENTS:

- 1 whole turkey, about 12-14 lbs / 5.4-6.4 kg
- 1/2 cup unsalted butter, softened / 115g unsalted butter, softened
- 2 tablespoons chopped fresh herbs (rosemary, thyme, sage) / 2 tablespoons chopped fresh herbs (rosemary, thyme, sage)
- Salt and pepper to taste / Salt and pepper to taste

INSTRUCTIONS:

1. Preheat your Kaloric Maxx Air Fryer Oven to 350°F (175°C) using the Rotisserie function.
2. Rinse the turkey inside and out, then pat dry with paper towels.
3. In a small bowl, mix together softened butter, chopped herbs, salt, and pepper.
4. Carefully loosen the skin over the turkey breast and spread half of the herb butter mixture under the skin.
5. Rub the remaining herb butter mixture over the outside of the turkey.
6. Skewer the turkey onto the rotisserie spit, securing it tightly with the forks.
7. Place the spit into the air fryer oven and cook for 3 hours, or until the internal temperature of the turkey reaches 165°F (75°C).
8. Let the turkey rest for 20-30 minutes before carving.
9. Carve the turkey and serve with your favorite sides.

NUTRITIONAL INFO (PER SERVING): Calories: 450 | Fat: 25g | Carbs: 0g | Protein: 55g

Kaloric Maxx Air Fryer Oven Functions Used: Rotisserie

Tip: Tent the turkey with foil if it starts to brown too quickly.

MOUTHWATERING AIR FRYER ROASTED BEEF TENDERLOIN

Prep: 10 mins | Cook: 25 mins | Serves: 6

INGREDIENTS:

- 2 lbs beef tenderloin, trimmed / 900g beef tenderloin, trimmed
- 2 tablespoons olive oil / 30ml olive oil
- 2 cloves garlic, minced / 2 cloves garlic, minced
- 1 tablespoon chopped fresh rosemary / 1 tablespoon chopped fresh rosemary
- Salt and pepper to taste / Salt and pepper to taste

INSTRUCTIONS:

1. Rub the beef tenderloin with olive oil, minced garlic, chopped rosemary, salt, and pepper.
2. Preheat your Kaloric Maxx Air Fryer Oven to 400°F (200°C) using the Rotisserie function.
3. Skewer the beef tenderloin onto the rotisserie spit, securing it tightly with the forks.
4. Place the spit into the air fryer oven and cook for 25 minutes, or until the internal temperature of the beef reaches your desired level of doneness (135°F (57°C) for medium-rare, 145°F (63°C) for medium).
5. Let the beef rest for 10 minutes before slicing.
6. Slice the beef tenderloin and serve with roasted vegetables or your favorite sides.

NUTRITIONAL INFO (PER SERVING): Calories: 300 | Fat: 15g | Carbs: 0g | Protein: 40g

Kaloric Maxx Air Fryer Oven Functions Used: Rotisserie

Tip: Use a meat thermometer to ensure your beef tenderloin is cooked to perfection.

HERB-CRUSTED AIR FRYER ROASTED LEG OF LAMB

Prep: 15 mins | Cook: 1 hour 30 mins | Serves: 6

INGREDIENTS:

- 1 leg of lamb, bone-in, about 4-5 lbs / 1.8-2.3 kg
- 4 cloves garlic, minced / 4 cloves garlic, minced
- 2 tablespoons fresh rosemary, chopped / 2 tablespoons fresh rosemary, chopped
- 2 tablespoons fresh thyme, chopped / 2 tablespoons fresh thyme, chopped
- 2 tablespoons olive oil / 30ml olive oil
- Salt and pepper to taste / Salt and pepper to taste

INSTRUCTIONS:

1. In a small bowl, mix together minced garlic, chopped rosemary, chopped thyme, olive oil, salt, and pepper to form a paste.
2. Rub the herb paste all over the leg of lamb, ensuring it's evenly coated.
3. Preheat your Kaloric Maxx Air Fryer Oven to 375°F (190°C) using the Rotisserie function.
4. Skewer the leg of lamb onto the rotisserie spit, securing it tightly with the forks.
5. Place the spit into the air fryer oven and cook for 1 hour 30 minutes, or until the internal temperature of the lamb reaches 145°F (63°C) for medium-rare or 160°F (71°C) for medium.
6. Let the lamb rest for 15-20 minutes before carving.
7. Carve the lamb and serve with roasted vegetables or your favorite sides.

NUTRITIONAL INFO (PER SERVING): Calories: 400 | Fat: 20g | Carbs: 0g | Protein: 50g

Kaloric Maxx Air Fryer Oven Functions Used: Rotisserie

Tip: For a crispy exterior, increase the temperature to 400°F (200°C) during the last 10 minutes of cooking.

TENDER AIR FRYER ROTISSERIE PORK LOIN

Prep: 10 mins | Cook: 1 hour | Serves: 4

INGREDIENTS:

- 2 lbs pork loin roast / 900g pork loin roast
- 2 tablespoons olive oil / 30ml olive oil
- 2 teaspoons smoked paprika / 2 teaspoons smoked paprika
- 1 teaspoon garlic powder / 1 teaspoon garlic powder
- 1 teaspoon onion powder / 1 teaspoon onion powder
- Salt and pepper to taste / Salt and pepper to taste

INSTRUCTIONS:

1. Rub the pork loin with olive oil, smoked paprika, garlic powder, onion powder, salt, and pepper.
2. Preheat your Kaloric Maxx Air Fryer Oven to 375°F (190°C) using the Rotisserie function.
3. Skewer the pork loin onto the rotisserie spit, securing it tightly with the forks.
4. Place the spit into the air fryer oven and cook for 1 hour, or until the internal temperature of the pork reaches 145°F (63°C).
5. Let the pork rest for 10 minutes before slicing.
6. Slice the pork loin and serve with your favorite sides.

NUTRITIONAL INFO (PER SERVING): Calories: 320 | Fat: 15g | Carbs: 0g | Protein: 45g

Kaloric Maxx Air Fryer Oven Functions Used: Rotisserie

Tip: To add extra flavor, marinate the pork loin in the seasoning mixture overnight.

CRISPY AIR FRYER ROASTED DUCK

Prep: 20 mins | Cook: 2 hours | Serves: 4

INGREDIENTS:

- 1 whole duck, about 5 lbs / 2.3 kg
- 2 teaspoons five-spice powder / 2 teaspoons five-spice powder
- 2 tablespoons honey / 30ml honey
- 2 tablespoons soy sauce / 30ml soy sauce
- 2 cloves garlic, minced / 2 cloves garlic, minced
- Salt and pepper to taste / Salt and pepper to taste

INSTRUCTIONS:

1. Score the duck skin in a crosshatch pattern, being careful not to cut into the meat.
2. In a small bowl, mix together five-spice powder, honey, soy sauce, minced garlic, salt, and pepper.
3. Rub the spice mixture all over the duck, ensuring it's well coated, and let it marinate for at least 1 hour, or overnight in the refrigerator.
4. Preheat your Kaloric Maxx Air Fryer Oven to 350°F (175°C) using the Rotisserie function.
5. Skewer the duck onto the rotisserie spit, securing it tightly with the forks.
6. Place the spit into the air fryer oven and cook for 2 hours, or until the skin is crispy and the internal temperature of the duck reaches 165°F (75°C).
7. Let the duck rest for 10-15 minutes before carving.
8. Carve the duck and serve with plum sauce or your favorite dipping sauce.

NUTRITIONAL INFO (PER SERVING): Calories: 450 | Fat: 30g | Carbs: 5g | Protein: 35g

Kaloric Maxx Air Fryer Oven Functions Used: Rotisserie

Tip: Prick the duck skin with a fork before cooking to allow the fat to render and the skin to crisp up.

JUICY AIR FRYER ROASTED CORNISH HENS

Prep: 15 mins | Cook: 1 hour | Serves: 2

INGREDIENTS:

- 2 Cornish hens, about 1.5 lbs each / 680g each
- 4 tablespoons butter, softened / 60g butter, softened
- 2 cloves garlic, minced / 2 cloves garlic, minced
- 1 tablespoon fresh rosemary, chopped / 1 tablespoon fresh rosemary, chopped
- 1 tablespoon fresh thyme, chopped / 1 tablespoon fresh thyme, chopped
- Salt and pepper to taste / Salt and pepper to taste

INSTRUCTIONS:

1. In a small bowl, mix together softened butter, minced garlic, chopped rosemary, chopped thyme, salt, and pepper.
2. Rub the butter mixture all over the Cornish hens, making sure to coat them evenly.
3. Preheat your Kaloric Maxx Air Fryer Oven to 375°F (190°C) using the Rotisserie function.
4. Skewer the Cornish hens onto the rotisserie spit, securing them tightly with the forks.
5. Place the spit into the air fryer oven and cook for 1 hour, or until the internal temperature of the hens reaches 165°F (75°C).
6. Let the Cornish hens rest for 5-10 minutes before serving.
7. Serve the Cornish hens whole or halved, with your favorite side dishes.

NUTRITIONAL INFO (PER SERVING): Calories: 550 | Fat: 35g | Carbs: 0g | Protein: 55g

Kaloric Maxx Air Fryer Oven Functions Used: Rotisserie

Tip: For extra flavor, baste the Cornish hens with the pan drippings halfway through cooking.

FLAVORFUL AIR FRYER ROTISSERIE RIB-EYE ROAST

Prep: 10 mins | Cook: 1 hour 30 mins | Serves: 4-6

INGREDIENTS:

- 3 lbs boneless rib-eye roast / 1.4 kg boneless rib-eye roast
- 2 tablespoons olive oil / 30ml olive oil
- 3 cloves garlic, minced / 3 cloves garlic, minced
- 2 teaspoons dried thyme / 2 teaspoons dried thyme
- 2 teaspoons dried rosemary / 2 teaspoons dried rosemary
- Salt and pepper to taste / Salt and pepper to taste

INSTRUCTIONS:

1. Rub the rib-eye roast with olive oil, minced garlic, dried thyme, dried rosemary, salt, and pepper.
2. Preheat your Kaloric Maxx Air Fryer Oven to 375°F (190°C) using the Rotisserie function.
3. Skewer the rib-eye roast onto the rotisserie spit, securing it tightly with the forks.
4. Place the spit into the air fryer oven and cook for 1 hour 30 minutes, or until the internal temperature of the roast reaches 135°F (57°C) for medium-rare or 145°F (63°C) for medium.
5. Remove the roast from the air fryer oven and let it rest for 15-20 minutes before slicing.
6. Slice the rib-eye roast and serve with your favorite side dishes.

NUTRITIONAL INFO (PER SERVING): Calories: 400 | Fat: 25g | Carbs: 0g | Protein: 45g

Kaloric Maxx Air Fryer Oven Functions Used: Rotisserie

Tip: For a crispy exterior, sear the roast in a hot skillet before skewering it onto the rotisserie spit.

SUCCULENT AIR FRYER ROASTED PRIME RIB

Prep: 20 mins | Cook: 2 hours | Serves: 6-8

INGREDIENTS:

- 4 lbs bone-in prime rib roast / 1.8 kg bone-in prime rib roast
- 4 cloves garlic, minced / 4 cloves garlic, minced
- 2 tablespoons olive oil / 30ml olive oil
- 2 tablespoons fresh rosemary, chopped / 2 tablespoons fresh rosemary, chopped
- 2 tablespoons fresh thyme, chopped / 2 tablespoons fresh thyme, chopped
- Salt and pepper to taste / Salt and pepper to taste

INSTRUCTIONS:

1. Preheat your Kaloric Maxx Air Fryer Oven to 375°F (190°C) using the Rotisserie function.
2. Make several small incisions all over the prime rib roast and insert the minced garlic into the incisions.
3. Rub the roast with olive oil, chopped rosemary, chopped thyme, salt, and pepper, ensuring it's well coated.
4. Skewer the prime rib roast onto the rotisserie spit, securing it tightly with the forks.
5. Place the spit into the air fryer oven and cook for 2 hours, or until the internal temperature of the roast reaches 135°F (57°C) for medium-rare or 145°F (63°C) for medium.
6. Remove the roast from the air fryer oven and let it rest for 15-20 minutes before slicing.
7. Slice the prime rib roast and serve with au jus and horseradish sauce.

NUTRITIONAL INFO (PER SERVING): Calories: 550 | Fat: 35g | Carbs: 0g | Protein: 55g

Kaloric Maxx Air Fryer Oven Functions Used: Rotisserie

Tip: Use a meat thermometer to ensure the roast reaches the desired level of doneness.

TENDER AIR FRYER ROTISSERIE TURKEY BREAST

Prep: 15 mins | Cook: 1 hour | Serves: 4-6

INGREDIENTS:

- 3 lbs boneless turkey breast / 1.4 kg boneless turkey breast
- 2 tablespoons olive oil / 30ml olive oil
- 2 teaspoons dried sage / 2 teaspoons dried sage
- 2 teaspoons dried thyme / 2 teaspoons dried thyme
- 2 teaspoons paprika / 2 teaspoons paprika
- Salt and pepper to taste / Salt and pepper to taste

INSTRUCTIONS:

1. Rub the turkey breast with olive oil, dried sage, dried thyme, paprika, salt, and pepper.
2. Preheat your Kaloric Maxx Air Fryer Oven to 375°F (190°C) using the Rotisserie function.
3. Skewer the turkey breast onto the rotisserie spit, securing it tightly with the forks.
4. Place the spit into the air fryer oven and cook for 1 hour, or until the internal temperature of the turkey breast reaches 165°F (75°C).
5. Remove the turkey breast from the air fryer oven and let it rest for 10-15 minutes before slicing.
6. Slice the turkey breast and serve with cranberry sauce and roasted vegetables.

NUTRITIONAL INFO (PER SERVING): Calories: 200 | Fat: 8g | Carbs: 0g | Protein: 30g

Kaloric Maxx Air Fryer Oven Functions Used: Rotisserie

Tip: Use a meat thermometer to ensure the turkey breast is cooked through but still moist.

HERB-CRUSTED AIR FRYER ROASTED RACK OF LAMB

Prep: 15 mins | Cook: 30 mins | Serves: 2-4

INGREDIENTS:

- 1 rack of lamb, frenched, about 1.5 lbs / 680g rack of lamb, frenched
- 2 tablespoons Dijon mustard / 30ml Dijon mustard
- 2 cloves garlic, minced / 2 cloves garlic, minced
- 2 tablespoons fresh rosemary, chopped / 2 tablespoons fresh rosemary, chopped
- 2 tablespoons fresh thyme, chopped / 2 tablespoons fresh thyme, chopped
- Salt and pepper to taste / Salt and pepper to taste

INSTRUCTIONS:

1. Preheat your Kaloric Maxx Air Fryer Oven to 375°F (190°C) using the Rotisserie function.
2. In a small bowl, mix together Dijon mustard, minced garlic, chopped rosemary, chopped thyme, salt, and pepper.
3. Rub the herb mixture all over the rack of lamb, coating it evenly.
4. Skewer the rack of lamb onto the rotisserie spit, securing it tightly with the forks.
5. Place the spit into the air fryer oven and cook for 25-30 minutes, or until the internal temperature of the lamb reaches 145°F (63°C) for medium-rare or 160°F (71°C) for medium.
6. Remove the rack of lamb from the air fryer oven and let it rest for 10 minutes before slicing.
7. Slice the rack of lamb into chops and serve with mint jelly or a red wine reduction.

NUTRITIONAL INFO (PER SERVING): Calories: 350 | Fat: 25g | Carbs: 2g | Protein: 28g

Kaloric Maxx Air Fryer Oven Functions Used: Rotisserie

Tip: Use a meat thermometer to ensure the lamb is cooked to your desired level of doneness.

SMOKY AIR FRYER ROTISSERIE HAM

Prep: 10 mins | Cook: 1 hour 30 mins | Serves: 6-8

INGREDIENTS:

- 4 lbs bone-in ham / 1.8 kg bone-in ham
- 1/4 cup brown sugar / 50g brown sugar
- 2 tablespoons Dijon mustard / 30ml Dijon mustard
- 1/4 cup pineapple juice / 60ml pineapple juice
- 1 teaspoon smoked paprika / 1 teaspoon smoked paprika
- 1/2 teaspoon ground cloves / 1/2 teaspoon ground cloves

INSTRUCTIONS:

1. In a small bowl, mix together brown sugar, Dijon mustard, pineapple juice, smoked paprika, and ground cloves to make the glaze.
2. Preheat your Kaloric Maxx Air Fryer Oven to 350°F (175°C) using the Rotisserie function.
3. Score the surface of the ham in a diamond pattern and brush the glaze all over the ham.
4. Skewer the ham onto the rotisserie spit, securing it tightly with the forks.
5. Place the spit into the air fryer oven and cook for 1 hour 30 minutes, basting the ham with the remaining glaze every 30 minutes.
6. Remove the ham from the air fryer oven and let it rest for 10-15 minutes before slicing.
7. Slice the ham and serve with your favorite sides like mashed potatoes or roasted vegetables.

NUTRITIONAL INFO (PER SERVING): Calories: 250 | Fat: 10g | Carbs: 12g | Protein: 30g

Kaloric Maxx Air Fryer Oven Functions Used: Rotisserie

Tip: Use a pastry brush to evenly coat the ham with the glaze for a caramelized finish.

HERB-CRUSTED AIR FRYER ROASTED SALMON

Prep: 10 mins | Cook: 15 mins | Serves: 4

INGREDIENTS:

- 4 salmon fillets, about 6 oz each / 170g each
- 2 tablespoons olive oil / 30ml olive oil
- 2 tablespoons fresh parsley, chopped / 2 tablespoons fresh parsley, chopped
- 2 tablespoons fresh dill, chopped / 2 tablespoons fresh dill, chopped
- 2 cloves garlic, minced / 2 cloves garlic, minced
- 1 tablespoon lemon juice / 15ml lemon juice
- Salt and pepper to taste / Salt and pepper to taste

INSTRUCTIONS:

1. Preheat your Kaloric Maxx Air Fryer Oven to 375°F (190°C) using the Rotisserie function.
2. In a small bowl, mix together olive oil, chopped parsley, chopped dill, minced garlic, lemon juice, salt, and pepper.
3. Rub the herb mixture over the salmon fillets, coating them evenly.
4. Skewer the salmon fillets onto the rotisserie spit, securing them tightly with the forks.
5. Place the spit into the air fryer oven and cook for 12-15
1. minutes, or until the salmon is cooked through and flakes easily with a fork.
6. Remove the salmon from the air fryer oven and let it rest for a few minutes before serving.
7. Serve the herb-crusted salmon with lemon wedges and your favorite side dishes.

NUTRITIONAL INFO (PER SERVING): Calories: 300 | Fat: 18g | Carbs: 2g | Protein: 32g

Kaloric Maxx Air Fryer Oven Functions Used: Rotisserie

Tip: Be sure not to overcook the salmon to keep it moist and flavorful.

FLAVORFUL AIR FRYER ROASTED ROOT VEGETABLES

Prep: 15 mins | Cook: 30 mins | Serves: 4-6

INGREDIENTS:

- 1 lb carrots, peeled and cut into sticks / 450g carrots, peeled and cut into sticks
- 1 lb parsnips, peeled and cut into sticks / 450g parsnips, peeled and cut into sticks
- 1 lb sweet potatoes, peeled and cut into chunks / 450g sweet potatoes, peeled and cut into chunks
- 2 tablespoons olive oil / 30ml olive oil
- 2 teaspoons dried thyme / 2 teaspoons dried thyme
- 2 teaspoons dried rosemary / 2 teaspoons dried rosemary
- Salt and pepper to taste / Salt and pepper to taste

INSTRUCTIONS:

1. Preheat your Kaloric Maxx Air Fryer Oven to 375°F (190°C) using the Rotisserie function.
2. In a large bowl, toss together the carrots, parsnips, and sweet potatoes with olive oil, dried thyme, dried rosemary, salt, and pepper until evenly coated.
3. Skewer the vegetables onto the rotisserie spit, arranging them evenly.
4. Place the spit into the air fryer oven and cook for 25-30 minutes, or until the vegetables are tender and golden brown, rotating the spit halfway through cooking.
5. Remove the roasted root vegetables from the air fryer oven and let them cool slightly before serving.
6. Serve the vegetables as a side dish or with a dipping sauce of your choice.

NUTRITIONAL INFO (PER SERVING): Calories: 150 | Fat: 7g | Carbs: 20g | Protein: 2g

Kaloric Maxx Air Fryer Oven Functions Used: Rotisserie

Tip: Cut the vegetables into uniform sizes to ensure even cooking.

CRISPY AIR FRYER ROASTED POTATOES

Prep: 10 mins | Cook: 30 mins | Serves: 4-6

INGREDIENTS:

- 2 lbs baby potatoes, halved / 900g baby potatoes, halved
- 2 tablespoons olive oil / 30ml olive oil
- 2 teaspoons garlic powder / 2 teaspoons garlic powder
- 2 teaspoons onion powder / 2 teaspoons onion powder
- 1 teaspoon smoked paprika / 1 teaspoon smoked paprika
- Salt and pepper to taste / Salt and pepper to taste

INSTRUCTIONS:

1. Preheat your Kaloric Maxx Air Fryer Oven to 375°F (190°C) using the Rotisserie function.
2. In a large bowl, toss together the halved baby potatoes with olive oil, garlic powder, onion powder, smoked paprika, salt, and pepper until evenly coated.
3. Skewer the seasoned potatoes onto the rotisserie spit, arranging them evenly.
4. Place the spit into the air fryer oven and cook for 25-30 minutes, or until the potatoes are crispy and golden brown, shaking the basket halfway through cooking.
5. Remove the roasted potatoes from the air fryer oven and let them cool slightly before serving.
6. Serve the crispy roasted potatoes as a side dish or with your favorite dipping sauce.

NUTRITIONAL INFO (PER SERVING): Calories: 180 | Fat: 7g | Carbs: 26g | Protein: 3g

Kaloric Maxx Air Fryer Oven Functions Used: Rotisserie

Tip: For extra crispy potatoes, parboil them for 5 minutes before seasoning and cooking.

CONCLUSION

As you've discovered throughout this cookbook, the Kaloric Maxx Air Fryer Oven is a true culinary powerhouse, opening up a world of possibilities for creating delicious, healthy, and convenient meals. From crispy appetizers and indulgent desserts to perfectly cooked proteins and vibrant vegetable dishes, this versatile appliance has proven itself to be an indispensable addition to any modern kitchen.

One of the most remarkable aspects of the Kaloric Maxx Air Fryer Oven is its ability to replicate the crispy, golden-brown texture of deep-fried foods with little to no oil. By harnessing the power of rapid air circulation and precise temperature control, you can enjoy all your favorite fried treats without the guilt or excessive fat and calories associated with traditional frying methods.

Beyond its air frying prowess, the Kaloric Maxx Air Fryer Oven shines as a multifunctional cooking marvel. Its rotisserie capabilities allow you to roast meats and vegetables to juicy perfection, while the dehydration function opens up a world of possibilities for creating homemade snacks, jerky, and fruit chips. The oven and baking settings enable you to tackle a wide range of recipes, from pizzas and breads to cakes and pastries, all with the convenience of a single appliance.

Throughout this cookbook, we've explored a diverse array of recipes that showcase the versatility and culinary potential of the Kaloric Maxx Air Fryer Oven. From mouthwatering appetizers and delectable breakfast dishes to satisfying vegetarian and vegan options, as well as elevated main courses featuring poultry, beef, pork, and seafood, there truly is something for every taste and dietary preference.

We've also delved into the art of air frying, providing you with valuable tips and tricks to help you master this healthy cooking technique. From proper preheating and basket loading techniques to essential cleaning and maintenance practices, you now have the knowledge and tools to achieve consistent, delicious results with every use.

As you continue your air frying journey, remember to embrace experimentation and let your culinary creativity soar. The recipes in this cookbook are merely a starting point – feel free to adapt them to suit your personal tastes and dietary needs, or use them as inspiration to create your own unique dishes.

Lastly, don't forget to share the joy of air frying with your loved ones. Whether you're hosting a casual gathering or a formal dinner party, the Kaloric Maxx Air Fryer Oven is sure to impress your guests with its ability to produce restaurant-quality meals right in your own kitchen.

Embrace the convenience, versatility, and healthful benefits of air frying, and let the Kaloric Maxx Air Fryer Oven be your trusty companion on a culinary journey filled with flavor, creativity, and nourishment.

Made in the USA
Columbia, SC
04 December 2024

48379102R00065